UFO CRASH IN BRAZIL

A Genuine UFO Crash with Surviving ETs

A thorough Investigation

by
Dr. Roger K. Leir

Published 2005
The Book Tree
San Diego, CA

ISBN 1-58509-105-7

Editors
Paul Tice and Mario Chavarria

Layout and Design
Atulya

Cover Art © by
Juan Cockburn

Published by
The Book Tree
P O Box 16476
San Diego, CA 92176

We provide fascinating and educational products to help awaken the public to new ideas and
information that would not be available otherwise.
Call 1 (800) 700-8733 for our *FREE BOOK TREE CATALOG*.

DEDICATION

To A. J. Gevaerd, Ubirajara Rodrigues and the many other hard working UFO researchers in Brazil who have given their time and energy toward bringing this information to the public. My deepest thanks is offered for their help and assistance in my own research.

Table of Contents

ACKNOWLEDGMENTS

I would like to thank Mario Rangel, from Sao Paulo, for his kindness, hospitality and help with my research. I thank the people of Brazil, and especially those from Varginha who were so kind and cooperative in my effort to perform the research in this case. If it were not for their help, this book and the investigation could not have been done.

Ubirajara Franco Rodrigues – Independent UFO Researcher and Chief investigator of the Varginha UFO Incident.

Bob Pratt – Independent USA UFO investigator and author.

Cynthia Luce – Brazilian UFO researcher.

A.J. Gevaerd – Editor of *UFO Magazine*, Brazil, and UFO researcher.

Claudeir Covo – Instituto Nacional de Investigacao de Fenomenos Aeroespacia.

Edison Boaventura Jr. and Jamil Vilanova, Grupo Ufologico do Guaruja, Sao Paulo.

Oswaldo and Eduardo Mondini, Centro de Pesquisas Exologicas, Sumare, Sao Paulo.

Centro Brasileiro de Pesquisas de Discos Voadores e Revista UFO O Campo Grande, Mato Grosso.

Marco Antonio Petit de Castro, Associacao Fluminense de Estudos Ufologicos, Itaipava, Rio de Janeiro.

Raphael Cury – Associacao Nacional dos Ufologos do Brasil, Curitiba, Parana.

Irene Granchi – Centro de Investigacao sobre a natureza dos Extraterrestras, Rio de Janeiro.

Marco Antonio Rodrigues Silva, Grupo de Estudos de Objetos nao Identificados, Sao Paulo.

Vitorio Pacaccini, Centro de Investigacao Civil de Objetos Aereos Nao Identificados, Belo Horizonte, Minas Gerais.

And yet... the future is still the uncertain future, and the alien mind is still mysteriously alien. We do not know their attitude toward our own humanity as it is now with most of earth's population as yet untouched by forced genet - ic manipulation. We do not know how the aliens view our inherent qualities of spirituality, physical diversity, romantic love, humor and sexuality. Or our intensely protective love for our children, our rich artistic expressiveness, and our willingness to sacrifice our own selves for the greater good. How many of these basic human qualities... do they truly envy and wish to append to their own narrow natures?

—Budd Hopkins, author of *Sight Unseen: Science, UFO Invisibility and Transgenic Beings*

PREFACE

It has been many years since I took my first steps into researching the UFO phenomenon. The journey has been long and hard. What I had not anticipated was the supreme elusiveness of the answers to the basic questions I was seeking. It would appear that the intelligence we are dealing with could at some point be considered comical in its approach to our endeavors. When I seemed to be close to acquiring answers to the questions I was seeking, I found instead more confusing data that raised even further questions. Despite all this, I am spurned by the sheer mysteriousness of the phenomenon. I have learned the nature of this form of phenomenology is not localized, but is worldwide. To this end it has been necessary for me to travel the globe, following leads like a trained bloodhound chasing the scent of his elusive victim.

Over the past years I have performed investigations in over twenty countries. Since my interest mainly lies in the physical evidence aspects of the subject, I have had to follow cases blindly in hope that such evidence will manifest. There were numerous times when it was only eyewitness testimony to an event that caught my interest. I have found, many times, that merely seeking out eyewitness accounts will lead to the highly sought after physical evidence. On many occasions other investigators had the first opportunity to obtain testimony and observe. I found this helped with my own personal endeavors due to the fact that many times a path was there for me to follow. Many of these cases required the help of local investigators due to language barriers. Without their help I would not have been able to proceed. Also, the results of the previous research would become important in my own efforts. A thorough review of this previous data many times has opened doors and allowed new leads to develop. It is always my hope to obtain the ultimate, which may be in the form actual physical material that could be sent to a laboratory for analysis. However I have found eyewitness testimony can be just as important as laboratory findings. Many times the conclusions I have drawn were derived from actual witnesses and used in conjunction with analytical evidence, such as documentation in the form of photographs or signed documents by military or government officials. One such set of documents came to my attention during one of my visits to Brazil. These particular documents pertain to agreements made between the American National Aviation and Space Administration (NASA) and the

8

Brazilian government. These agreements were signed by prominent individuals from both countries and reference the sharing of information between the two countries. They allow for the material coming from space that is found in Brazil to be turned over to the government of the United States, and then both parties agree to share the reverse engineering data and benefits. In this text I intend to demonstrate how these agreements affect the material in the Varginha, Brazil, crashed saucer case.

I am also sure such written agreements exist with other countries than Brazil. This does not mean that every single country or government on the face of this planet have such agreements with the U.S. In fact, it is possible that the majority have little or no knowledge of the extraterrestrial situation at all. It is also my opinion that not all parts of a complex government system share the information equally. Even in the U.S. there may be numerous government establishments who are not privy to the classified information. The question of who actually has this knowledge and who doesn't is a difficult one to answer. Perhaps there is a worldwide secret group that is the controlling overseer of the knowledge and it in turn shares with only those who are allowed into the secret Cabal.

Other forms of documentation also include medical records and medical evidence. A classic example is the biological evidence, which is gleaned in animal mutilations as well as animal and human predator cases. The chuparacabra phenomenon has involved numerous medical and biological documents, which should be considered vitally important to the research in general. In conclusion, it is my opinion that the secrets of this complex phenomenon will only be unlocked by *following the science.*

FOREWORD
by
Marcos Malvezzi Leal

I believe most UFO investigators will agree that Brazil has one of the richest, most colorful histories in UFO activity around the globe. Even before the so-called "modern era" of flying saucers began, when American pilot Kenneth Arnold first coined the expression "Flying Saucer" after his sightings over the Rocky Mountains, close encounters of the second and third kind were happening in both city and countryside areas.

In fact, a pioneering UFO researcher in Brazil, Ms. Irene Granchi, relates the story of a man and his wife who were awakened in the middle of the night by a strange luminosity that penetrated their bedroom through the windowpanes. As there was no electricity in the neighborhood, both were immediately frightened and looked out the window to check on the source of the eerie light. The husband had picked up his shotgun and set to fire. What they saw scared them out of their wits. A large ball-shaped object hovered above the ground at close range to the couple's little house. Both described the "thing" as a one-legged tall monster, shining all over and absolutely silent, with large "squared" and black eyes. To the modern UFO researcher, the apparition would turn out to be a round or oval-shaped craft with square portholes, while the "leg" was probably the typical light cone often projected down from hovering UFOs. The bullets fired from the frightened man's shotgun seemed to ricochet and have no effect on the monster... but it eventually elevated from the ground and disappeared. This was in the early 1930's.[1]

In another important incident, which occurred in 1947, Brazilian topographer José Higgins was working in the fields of a small rural community in the state of Paraná. He heard a sharp humming sound overhead and immediately looked up. Completely astounded, he saw a circular-shaped object descending smoothly from the sky. His party of laborers quickly dispersed, as the men were frightened out of their wits, leaving Higgins alone. The strange craft circled around and eventually landed at a distance from his working spot. It was about 100 feet wide and surrounded by a series of metal tubes, from which he thought the humming sound was coming. From its lower part, a kind of door opened and three beings came out wearing what seemed, to Higgin, like trunks and shirts. They were tall and big, with large eyes. As they approached, the witness realized they had no eyelashes. Their heads were a little bit larger than ours, even in proportion to their large bodies. Higgins noticed, through the opening in the bottom part of the craft, that there were more men inside the UFO. The aliens moved about Higgins and began to talk to each other in an unintelligible language. One of them gestured to him, indicating he wanted him to get inside the craft. Higgins asked where they would take him, but oral communication was obviously impossible. Discreetly, he began to back down and eventually ran and hid behind some bushes. The aliens seemed to take no further interest in him. Apparently, they were playing around like kids, jumping and tossing stones around. After about half an hour, they stopped this charade, went back into the object the same way they had come out. The UFO produced the same humming sound and lifted off, disappearing into the clouds. The case was thoroughly researched by the now extinct Sociedade Brasileira de Pesquisa de Discos Voadores (Brazilian Society for the Research of Flying Saucers).

There are many famous Brazilian cases. From the famous sighting over Trindade Island of a Saturn-shaped UFO, photographed by Almiro Baraúna aboard the navy vessel *Almirante Saldanha*, to the internationally renowned case of Antonio Villas Boas, who was taken aboard a landed alien craft and forced to copulate with a female extraterrestrial entity (both incidents occurred in 1950s). The menu is long and varied, and the veracity of many of the accounts is confirmed by both Brazilian and foreign researchers, UFO study groups, as well as professionals of the most varied fields.

By far, the most astounding incident involving UFOs and alien creatures in Brazil was the incident in the town of Varginha (in the state of Minas Gerais) in 1996, in which two alien beings were captured by the military. The story, of course, was quickly hushed and the three main witnesses were even bribed with money by unknown men to withdraw their story, go public and tell people they had, in fact, seen nothing. The honesty of all witnesses involved, coupled with the strange comings and goings of military vehicles in and out of the area, made many suspicious. These vehicles were said to be carrying bags that seemingly contained a "precious cargo" which was deposited at the local military bases. This was compounded by the testimony of some military authorities that obviously wished to remain unidentified. These facts were enough to convince the renowned Brazilian investigator, Ubirajara Franco Rodrigues, that a UFO had actually crashed in the area and two of its occupants had managed to survive and, though perhaps badly hurt, roamed about the neighborhood, ending up in the hands of the military.[2]

The Varginha Incident is the main subject matter of this book, which Dr. Roger K. Leir is now presenting to the public. I am honored to have become familiar with Dr. Leir's prior research on extraterrestrial implants detected in the bodies of abductees when I was assigned to translate his book *The Aliens and the Scalpel*, 2nd Edition, into Portuguese for publication in Brazil by Brazilian UFO Magazine (edited by Mr. A. J. Gevaerd).[3] Later, I had the privilege of meeting him in person when he visited Brazil in 2002 and 2003. I interpreted for him at two International Congresses, held in the city of Curitiba, capital of the State of Paraná. I also accompanied him in interviews and even a city tour. He is not only a jolly companion on side trips and dinners, but also a terrific, insightful talker. He is a magnificent writer, describing sometimes long and technical procedures in a way that is easily accessible to the general public. His style is sober and thorough. His lectures in Curitiba were absolutely enthralling, and when you hear him, you are struck by the seriousness in which he conducts his research.

Now the public is once again presented with an extraordinary work that is sure to affect everyone's views about extraterrestrial visitation and the convenient manipulation by authorities that wish to keep us in the dark. This is definitely a book that will add an enormous contribution both to Ufology in general, and to the public awareness of UFO activity around the world.

Marcos Malvezzi Leal is the translations coordinator for Brazilian *UFO Magazine* and author of *Seres, Fantástica Realidade* [*Beings, Fantastic Reality*], published by Editora 21, São Paulo, Brasil, 2003.

---

1. Irene Granchi, *UFOs e abducoes no Brasil*, Novo Milenio Publishers, Rio de Janeiro (RJ), 1992.

2. Ubirajara F. Rodrigues' book, *O Caso Varginha*, was published by Centro Brasileiro de Pesquisas de Discos Voadores (CBPDV) and Grupo Editorial Paracientífico (GEP), Campo Grande (MS), 2000.

3. Published in Brazil as *Implantes Alienígenas*, by Centro de Pesquisas de Discos Voadores (CBPDV) and Grupo Editorial Paracientífico (GEP), Campo Grande (MS), 2002.

Chapter 1

BRAZIL
THE LAND OF UFOs

It has been said that Brazil is a land of exotic collision. Cows lumber across multi-lane highways and at the same time, the sounds of battery energized TV sets can be heard blaring away in the surrounding jungle. All this, coupled with some of the world's most sophisticated music wafting from its sorriest ghettoes, sets the scene for the modern day surrealistic scenes of Brazil. When this is contrasted with the sights of the more modern metropolises with skyscrapers surging like icons toward heaven, only blocks away from beaches with the most incredible beauty, you really get the feeling of stepping into paradise. If you like heat and humidity you have also come to the right part of the world. However, the term hot has many applications. I found hot spices, hot rhythms, and the heat of the moment all blended together, producing a cultural mélange that favors mystics and marketplaces; and yet, just a few miles away are cold winters, sauerkraut, and European-style beer fests. Brazil can be considered by some to be a third-world country with a first-world face; a persona that often tricks not only it's own native people, but in addition, the unsuspecting visitor. Long called a sleeping giant, Brazil is just now wiggling its gargantuan toes and waking from hibernation that has, with a few notable exceptions, kept it politically and economically dazed for most of the twentieth century. As the biggest country in South America, Brazil boasts some of the greatest wealth and the greatest inequality in the entire world—at times, even the sunshine seems unfairly distributed.

Brazil's place in the South American continent is represented by more than just a large section of this world's landmass, it also represents the most populated county in Latin America, boasting a population of over 150 million people. It also has another interesting geographic feature in that it borders every country in South America with the exception of Ecuador and Chile. It should also be noted that forty-five percent of the total population could be found in the southern regions, which represent only 14% of the territory. The Amazon rainforest occupies about 42% of the total landmass, although it represents home to fewer people than live in New York City.

Despite the construction of the most modern capital of Brasilia, which has been built on the central plateau, the population remains sparse.

Perhaps it comes as no surprise that Brazil has also gained a worldwide reputation for some of the most famous international UFO sightings

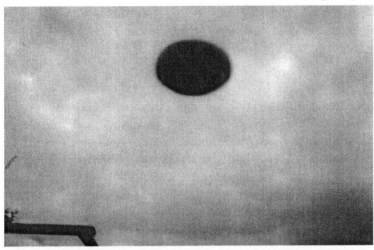

Clear photos taken of UFOs in Brazil,
one in the daytime, one at night.

I have traveled to this South American land of enchantment many times over the past several years at the request of the South American UFO research community, which has taken great interest in my work with the alien abduction phenomena. I felt it a personal honor and privilege to be considered an equal colleague with this prestigious group of investigators. My visits to this country have afforded me the opportunity to see more of the country than the average North American tourist. I have found most of the larger cities in Brazil contain the same qualities found in cities all over the world. Since I am not personally fond of large city environments, my views may be very biased. Seeing humanity crowded into small geographical areas, producing pollution through the use of fossil fuels, artificially converting the landscape into ribbons of asphalt, polluting the water supply and covering the terrain with human manufactured by-products does not represent what I think mankind's destiny should be for this planet. It is not that I have singled out Brazil for this criticism. In fact, it should win an award for having fewer cities fitting the aforementioned description than most other countries.

One of my favorite cities in Brazil is the very first community I visited. The city of Curitiba is south of Sao Paulo and lies about 50 miles from the coast. From Sao Paulo by air it takes about an hour and a half; by automobile, the time is extended to anywhere from eight to ten hours of driving, depending on the traffic. However, it is a wonderful opportunity to see the lush Brazilian countryside. The roads are good and in many places, comparable to highways in the U.S. The traffic varies from very light to heavy, depending on the time of day. Portions of the highway are only two lanes and this can produce delays, as it is difficult to pass the myriad of trucks traveling the roads. I was fortunate to have a Brazilian colleague with me who had negotiated one of these thoroughfares many times previously. I found it interesting to note that the foot traffic we passed, which consisted of large numbers of individuals, both male and female, walked along the shoulder of the road. Many were carrying large parcels or what appeared to be shopping bags. My companion explained that some walk many miles to do their shopping. What I found strange was the absence of houses or structures for many miles along the same areas where we saw heavy pedestrian traffic. Again, my companion advised me that a closer look would reveal numerous small side trails that lead into the thick jungle foliage. In addition, he explained that they lead to habitats where this very poor segment of the population resides. This exemplifies what I consider to be the Brazilian enigma—a country in which the most modern portions of civilization are mixed with their own quaint, ancient ways.

I found the city of Curitiba to be modern by U.S. standards. It has an interesting history. It was founded in 1693 as a gold-mining camp. In 1853 the city became the capital of the state of Parana. The population has increased from 140,000 in 1940 to over 1.5 million today. It is truly an international city, with inhabitants settling in the area from Poland, Italy, Germany and Greece. Today, many come from all over the world to eventually settle in

Curitiba. The city is divided into numerous sections, each replete with it's own European culture. Of course, with this diversity of culture springs forth a fantastic variety of restaurants. Dining in Brazil in general is one of the great marvels of the world. If you like to eat then Brazil is the place to go. One of the unique forms of Brazilian dining is a style of restaurant called a churrascaria. Many of these are large and can serve about 1000 people at once. I learned if my taste was for beef, then a churrascaria was the place I wanted to be. I should also add that it is not only the quality of the beef, which is the best I have ever tasted, but also the very large assortment of side dishes. Tomatoes appear large and look as if they have been artificially colored a deep red color. Their taste tickles the tongue buds. This is also true with the taste and aroma of other fresh fruits and vegetables.

Many areas of Brazil are known hot spots for UFO activity and the city of Curitiba is no exception. Cities such as Sugar Loaf (Rio), Sao Tome das Letras and Sao Lourenco (Minas Gerais), Chapada dos Guimaraes, Mato Grosso, Alta Floresta Mato Grosso, and the Amazon Jungle are popular spots listed in many guide books for travelers in Brazil. One example is a 740-page guide to travel in Brazil called *Brazil Up Close*, written by Pamela Bloom.

The purpose for my initial visit to Curitiba was to present my research on the alien implant subject to both the Brazilian researchers and the public. The conference was held at a venue capable of seating about three hundred and there were approximately two hundred and fifty attendees. During the intermissions between speakers, many gathered in a large courtyard outside the main doors of the venue for refreshments and discussions pertaining to the conference. Although I did not understand or speak the native language, which is Portuguese, I was able to communicate with my limited knowledge of Spanish and the help of interpreters. There were times when I was surrounded by crowds of fifteen to twenty people, all gathering to ask questions about the UFO and alien abduction phenomena. Many of these individuals had not discussed their private experiences with another single living soul. The reason for this in Brazil is simply due to the fact there is no one to confer with. It was a very unique and emotional experience to observe individuals who were going through severe, disturbing gyrations with outbursts of tears, facial contortions and other abnormal psychological states. I found myself overwhelmed by sincere individuals who were undergoing similar psychological turmoil as those who were residents of the U.S. What was commonly written about in books on the subject of abduction by such noted authors as Budd Hopkins, Dr. John Mack and David Jacobs became the reality of the moment. For the first time I found myself an eyewitness to a phenomena which was obviously happening worldwide.

During my stay in Curitiba I had the privilege of being shown firsthand the sites where numerous UFO events had taken place, including a very beautiful park where eyewitnesses saw an abduction occur in broad daylight. Another memorable event occurred during an afternoon stroll with my colleagues down one of the busy downtown avenues. The weather was perfect and the beauty of the city stood out like a diamond. This was a wide cobblestone street in the downtown area, closed off to auto travel. The streets were spotlessly clean, and the variety of stores and little shops were more numerous than I had ever seen in one shopping area before. Ahead and to our right was what appeared to be a statue of white alabaster, attracting a small crowd of people. This site caught my eye and stirred my curiosity. Our group approached and I stopped to look at the detail of the sculpture. There was something about its appearance that just didn't look correct, but I couldn't put my finger on it. Suddenly I understood my feelings. I looked in amazement as the statue began to slowly move. It was not a statue at all, but a very clever mime dressed in a costume. Once he was fully animated the small gathering applauded, cheered and tossed coins into a large metal receptacle sitting on the street in front of the figure.

Our small group continued slowly down this interesting avenue. There was an immeasurable level of excitement in the atmosphere. The scene was composed of beautiful small shops, crowds of shoppers who were laughing and openly having a great time, smells of fresh bakery goods were everywhere, and along the sidewalk were cafes with patrons dining at curbside tables.

Without warning I heard a scream from behind me. I turned to see what was going on, along with the other members of our group. A few feet behind us I saw a young girl lying on the street, apparently in a state of acute distress. A small group of individuals were tending to her needs. I ran over to her and offered assistance. She could not speak English. I inquired of one of the bystanders who understood English about the problem. He calmly explained to me that the girl lying on the ground was having an acute panic attack because she saw a clown coming down the street. She evidently had an uncontrollable fear of clowns. Since most of the individuals I was with were either researchers in the UFO field or attendees at the conference, I was able to obtain the reason for this girl's fears. It turned out she was a victim of the alien abduction phenomena since early childhood. Her abductors had implanted a clown scenario in her memories in which they appeared as clowns. The events of the abductions were not pleasant and this poor, tortured soul was forced to carry these memories with her since childhood. I communicated with her as best as I could. She finally was able to sit up and continue with our group. I stayed with her for some time so I might be in a position to warn her if I saw another clown. One of my fellow researchers explained that clowns were common in this area of the city, since they entertained the crowds daily.

In my vast reading of the abduction literature I had recalled cases similar to this one. Budd Hopkins had written several times about abduction scenarios where their abductors had installed false memories into their victims, offering up memories of clowns, doctors, and animals with large eyes such as owls and deer. However this was the first time I had the opportunity to actually witness the reactions of an abductee while confronting one of their fears. It was far from a pleasant scene, and it will be ingrained into my memory for the rest of my life.

I have been back to Curitiba many times and each time I have met people with interesting stories relative to these phenomena. Some have been abductees, others have witnessed flying craft they could not recognize, and still others relate tales of landings and confrontations with UFO occupants. I have found the stories related to me by the Brazilians have little differences than descriptions coming from other countries. The craft reported are saucer shaped, triangular, cigar shaped, barrel-like, oval, round, and all without conventional aircraft characteristics such as a propulsion source, wings, vertical tail or other characteristics we have come to know as "conventional aircraft". The occupants or abductors are also described similarly to other places in the world. They describe beings that are short, gray in color, thin in stature, with large heads and big upturned black eyes. These we have come to know as "the grays". They also have described other beings as appearing human, with blonde hair, perfect features, tall and good-looking. In addition, there are descriptions of beings that appear insectoid, others appear short, with brown oily skin, disproportionate large heads and large, red, upturned eyes. There are also descriptions of other beings who are seen in some of the more remote areas such as the Amazon Jungle.

The relationship between Brazilians and these beings is also wide and varied. It has been reported that some people actually develop friendly bonds with these non-terrestrials, but some are not so fortunate. Most UFO literature does not mention the horror stories coming from areas such as Brazil. Terrible events are happening to some of the more primitive elements of this world's humanity. These are not discussed, even within the investigative portion of the UFO community. One such story I investigated was that of a family in the Brazilian jungle, financially poor, but rich in spirit and a zeal for living. A series of events occurred with this family that for many would seem similar to other typical alien visitation or abduction scenarios. In this case, the exception was that the abductors told their victim they were going to remove his eyes and this procedure would help them further the health of the world's population. This poor man totally accepted their explanation. He awoke the next morning blind. His eyes had been removed in total. He was not upset and it was only on the insistence of other family members that he consented to seek the opinion of a qualified ophthalmologist. It will probably not come as a surprise that the doctor did not believe his story and told one of his relatives that whomever removed the eyes were a very skilled surgeon and did a magnificent job. This is only one example of numerous stories coming from the more primitive areas of Brazil. There are cases of human mutilation that go without any publicity whatsoever. It should not surprise the reader to also learn that the United States has had cases involving some non-human intelligence that has perpetrated these sinister acts upon the U.S. population. If the truth were told to the public, it goes without saying there would be an uncontrollable panic.

Brazil is a large country with a marvelous history. The recorded UFO portion of it appears both written and told, with stories coming from tribal peoples. There are some additional cities involved that I have not mentioned. For example, Foz Do Iguaco (on the southeastern tip of the country in the state of Pantanal, which joins Argentina and Paraguay), Fortaleza (in the extreme northeast, in the state of Ceara and on the coast), Campo Grande (in the western-central region in the state of Mato Grosso) and Varginha (northwest of Sao Paulo, in the state of Minas Gerais).

I have personally visited many of these cities and shall be discussing important cases relative to these areas later in future chapters.

Chapter 2

THE GREAT BRAZILIAN HOAX

Numerous UFO stories have come out of Brazil over an extended period of time. Many have been thoroughly investigated by numerous qualified Brazilian investigators. Some of the more famous cases have warranted worldwide attention, thereby resulting in an influx of researchers from around the world. They performed their own personal inquiries and rendered opinions based on their findings. As in many other countries some cases of reported UFOs, including all their ramifications, fall into the category of ordinary, mundane terrestrial events. With these are a small portion of cases which have been shown to be purposeful hoaxes. It always amazes me that individuals will apply enormous amounts of time and effort in an attempt to fool a small number people. One of the examples is illustrated by the crop circle phenomena in the United Kingdom. At one time two individuals came forth and made statements to the effect that they had made the entire batch of crop circles—hence the Doug and Dave myth. Two portions of their preposterous hoax are deemed prime examples. The first portion demonstrates the use of partial truth. Yes, some crop configurations were indeed made by Doug and Dave. They were made very carefully over a protracted period of time and did fool a certain number of people, including some of the crop circle investigators. Number two involves both the intentional and non-intentional spread of the information. When the news of Doug and Dave's exploits hit the media, the information was used for a multiplicity of purposes. It played right into the hands of the disinformation specialists. It proved to the public at large that *all* crop circles were simply man-made configurations and certainly of terrestrial origin. From this point on, this hoax was passed through media channels worldwide, giving the impression that one should not look towards the subject of crop configurations with other than a slanted eye.

Hoaxers such as Doug and Dave, no matter what their personal intentions, were lucky in that they were able to use this Santa Claus-like tale to fool large segments of the population. Even so, if we look closely at what they had done, it should be noted that there was no particular harm done to anyone. We can also safely say that there was no particular act of criminality, other than trespassing into a farmer's field and destroying some of his crops. This puts the harm potential very low on the scale. The same can be said of those who perpetrate hoaxes by tossing hubcaps into the air and filming them, claiming them as genuine UFOs. Who does this really harm? UFO investigators are far and few between and to fool a few of them are rather minor in the face of the entire scheme of things. I am of the opinion that most hoaxes in the field of Ufology involve faking photographic evidence, and perhaps a minor amount involves attempts to fake landing evidence. It is a fact—many individuals with no malicious intent also perform *unintentional* hoaxes in this subject area. Many truly believe they may have seen something unusual flying in the skies, having witnessed terrestrial or man-made phenomena but, unfortunately, do not have the knowledge for a clear identification or an in-depth understanding.

There are a few instances where hoaxing in this area can result in harm to the individuals involved or to those who are actually fooled. It goes without saying that examples of this are demonstrated by such cults as "Heavens Gate" or "Jonestown", which resulted in the unfortunate deaths of many individuals. The case of the following Brazilian hoax contains the same terrible elements of potential destruction to human beings.

The Urnadir Hoax

The setting for this case takes place in a very small town in Brazil called Corguinho, which is in the State of Mata Grosso, do Sul. This tiny municipality is about two hours from one of the largest cities in the area, Campo Grande. The central story revolves around a supposed Brazilian businessman, Urandir Fernandes de Oliveira and his UFO sect called Projeto Portal (Gateway Project). All one has to do is enter the name Urandir into any search engine on the Internet and they will be rewarded with numerous pages relative to this man's claims.

In an effort to reduce this tale to the briefest and most concise form, I will try and stay with the most pertinent portions of the story. Urandir, who is 39 years of age, has stated to the world at large the he was abducted from his bedroom by alien beings and returned some three days later. He has offered up some proof of his claims. One such item is a bed sheet supposedly taken from the bed he was sleeping on at the time of his encounter. The bed sheet comes complete with an apparent burn mark, which depicts an outline of a human figure with the right arm extended. In addition to this, he has photographed a similar burn mark on the wood ceiling of the same room. Urandir has also stated that the very same night this event happened to him, small round stones fell miraculously from the sky. His very close friend, Felipe Branco, has confirmed Urandir's story and stated, "Many dozens of round rocks fell from the sky for about ten seconds while I was driving to the Corguinho farm on September 15, 2002 at around 7:30 P.M. local time."

Mr. Urandir Oliveira was born and raised in Sao Paulo, southwest of Rio de Janeiro. Some of his family moved on to a small farm in Campo Grande where he frequently visits. In the 1990s, Mr. Oliveira began telling people that extraterrestrial beings were coming (in their crafts) to a particular valley 100 kilometers beyond the town of Campo Grande. He also stated that he first encountered tall, blonde-haired "extraterrestrials" in 1976 when he was thirteen years old in the countryside of Sao Paulo. These Scandinavian-like entities took him into a craft and placed objects in his neck. He was told by these beings that the objects were to facilitate communication and interaction between him and the beings in the future.

In October of 1998 he stated that his second abduction occurred in Campo Grande, near a flat field with an adjoining hill or mesa. He also stated that approximately 70 people were witnesses to the event. The story is that he supposedly had contacted a number of Brazilian UFO researchers, as he was instructed to do by the extraterrestrials, so he could be seen being taken up into one of their crafts.

Mr. Oliveira's third abduction allegedly took place on September 15th of 2002. This purported event is really what put Mr. Oliveira on the international map. According to Urandir, the event took place around 7:30 PM. He was supposedly gone from his environment until September 18th, when he was returned at approximately 9 PM. The night of the 15th is when Felipe Branco states the rocks fell from the sky on to his car as he was approaching Urandir's home. Also according to Mr. Branco, he was unable to find Urandir in his bedroom, but instead found what appeared to be a burn mark in the shape of Urandir's body imprinted into the bed sheet. He also looked up and found a similar outline on the wooden ceiling. He stated that Urandir was nowhere to be found. According to Felipe, he and some friends, about 27 in number, then sealed off the bedroom and applied metal bars to the windows. The reason for this was never made exactly clear. When Urandir was mysteriously returned he attempted to escape the room but could not get out, as the door had been sealed and bars prevented his exit through the windows. Finally, after a desperate call on his compound's telephone communication system, he was able to summon help and was freed by his friends. It is Urandir's contention that a beam of violet light pierced his bedroom ceiling and lifted him off of his bed. He floated upward in this strange beam, passed through the ceiling and into the hovering craft above. Upon arrival into the craft he was placed in a transparent cylinder. The cylinder was closed and filled with a strange smoke. Urandir stated that he remembers standing in the craft, dressed in a strange nylon jumpsuit. He also stated he recalls tall humanoid beings wearing jumpsuits that glowed like neon lights. He was then given a demonstration, which showed one of the cylinders he was in filling with the smoke—and a jump suit materializing before his eyes.

Next he was taken to a large room with other beings who gave him information and showed him some of the ship's apparatus, including a large television-like screen. He described a variety of beings, some short and hairy, taller blondes, some with red hair, others with red hair and a few with chocolate colored skin.

When asked what he was shown on the television screen, he explained that he was able to see images of the earth having undergone some devastation from a meteor that entered our solar system and affected our electromagnetic field, causing a pole shift. He was shown that the effects were not as much as you might imagine. There were also images of rocks made of ice falling to earth. The time period at which these events would take place was between the years 2003 and 2012. Urandir also stated he was told about a microbiological war, either taking place in the future or already underway. When he asked about extraterrestrial intervention, he was told that they have difficulty interacting with us due to the difference in our vibrational frequencies.

Next he stated that he was taken to another area where an implant was placed in the back of his neck. The purpose for this device was to facilitate communication and interaction. He then claimed to have x-ray films showing three glowing objects in his neck. I have asked several of the researchers if they had seen these films and all have replied in the negative. I made numerous attempts to acquire the x-rays from many different sources but to no avail.

Urandir's life comes complete with other abduction events. As I mentioned previously, he stated his second abduction occurred in 1998. Supposedly the ETs had informed him they were going to show up at a specific place and time. The place, of course, was on his compound, which consists of 209 acres of farmland. He claims to have collected a crowd of about 70 people to witness the event, and in addition called a television crew from Brazil Verade TV, who were there with cameras rolling. Urandir also stated that a small beam of light descended from the ship, surrounding him and lifting him into a disc shaped craft. The videotaped evidence of this strange event mysteriously disappeared and was never shown on any TV program. There were no witnesses who were willing to come forward and verify that this event ever happened.

During this abduction Urandir stated that tall blonde beings showed him wall screen images of Earth's destruction by nuclear missiles and explosions of nuclear power reactors. He was told that the changing magnetic fields of the Earth would cause this event to happen by effecting the electronic systems of missiles and reactors. He stated that the blonde beings also showed him three fully functional pyramids currently covered by sand. At a later date these structures would be uncovered for the world to see.

The stories produced by Urandir in this case are fascinating and are reported to have been witnessed by credible individuals. Is it possible the story is genuine? Let's take a look at the next series of events.

Now comes the Brazilian UFO research community and one of Brazil's most respected researchers, A.J. Geveard, publisher of Brazil's most widely circulated magazine, Revista UFO.

Geveard, in a "Dear Colleague" letter to Brazilian UFO groups, presented a completely different picture of Urandir and his group, which is called Project Portal. In his letter dated November 28, 2001, Gevaerd stated, "Urandir was publicly exposed five years ago as probably the all-time most successful UFO hoaxer in the entire world."

It seems that Mr. Oliviera (founder of "Project Portal") and his group have been relentlessly criticized in Brazil for their fanatic behavior. Gevaerd also stated, "Project Portal has become the largest UFO cult in the world today." The mere knowledge of this stirs my emotions and has generated distinct memories of dead bodies lying on the ground at "Jonestown"; it also made me reflect on the TV pictures of the deceased individuals filmed inside the rooms at "Heavens Gate". Is it possible that a cult like "Project Portal", if allowed to continue in its existence, will also result in similar deaths? The answer in my opinion is an unqualified, YES!

Shortly after Urandir's last abduction story started gaining notoriety, the Brazilian research community contacted me. Because of the extended periods of time I had spent in Brazil, I had gained their trust. The first to notify me was A. J. Gevaerd, who went to great lengths to inform me about the background of Urandir. He explained that Urandir and his group of enthusiasts, "Project Portal", have been relentlessly criticized in Brazil for their fanatic behavior. In addition, he stated this organization has become the largest UFO cult in the world. It seems Urandir and his colleagues have gathered a sizable fortune in money and properties with their hoaxes. Gevaerd told me that Urandir and his associates charge high prices for folks to visit his "farm". It is estimated that over 50,000 people have visited, and more than 200,000 have attended his so-called "contact classes" in many parts of

Brazil. During these sessions he was caught red-handed using laser pointers and specialized lighting to fool his guests.

It was also brought to my attention that in March of the year 2000 Urandir and an associate were arrested and jailed in Porto Alegre for selling farmland that did not belong to them. Upwards of 6000 people were told by him that they would be safe from Armageddon and rescued be ETs if they purchased the land and moved to the property. Unfortunately, they never saw a piece of it.

To add insult to injury, it has been reported that over 900 visitors dished out over $400.00 to camp at an area of "Project Portal" where bathroom facilities were clogged to the point where sewage overflow had invaded the lodging areas. It was also found that the food was prepared with polluted water produced from a dam constructed on the property. His guests were asked to bathe in the artificial lake and, while doing so, Urandir asked the sky above to bless them and treat them for their evils if they would only have faith. If the person had little faith, the charm and prayer would not work.

Strange becomes Stranger

There is no way in the world I could have predicted what was about to happen next. I was shocked to learn that one of the world's most respected UFO researchers was announcing to the public that she had spent time with Urandir and considered his case to be the genuine article. Linda Moulton Howe has been researching in the field for many years. She has written numerous books and is particularly well known for her work with cattle mutilations. In addition, she has always been considered the epitome of honesty and has used science to the benefit of all. Why then would she take the time to investigate a case of such obvious fraud? Could it be because Urandir paid for all her expenses to travel to Brazil? Could it be that in her quest for knowledge and the desire to clear up the mystery of this case, she unwittingly bit off more than she could chew? Linda was able to interview a number of Urandir's closest associates, but for some reason she totally ignored and neglected to talk with anyone from the Brazilian UFO research community—at least any of those from the respected network that I had previously made contact with. She was given the now famous bed sheet to submit for analysis along with some of the stones reported to have fallen from the sky. She photographed the ceiling of the room where the abduction took place and placed photos of all the material she had gathered on her website. When I saw the photos of these stones I was shocked, as I had been given a number of them to take home with me many years ago. The stones I was given were exact replicas of what she had depicted on the website. I was told that these stones were commonly found in many areas of Brazil. Linda then appeared on several well-known radio shows announcing to the world that the case was genuine, even before there was a scientific investigation of the material she had acquired.

During the time of Linda's initial involvement, the Brazilian researchers became more vocal and stated they were shocked about her actions in defiance of their knowledge and research into the case. This resulted in continuous debate about the subject amongst the inner UFO circles, including the well-recognized MUFON (Mutual UFO Network) organization. To make matters even more complex, actual battle lines were drawn. Linda had been asked to speak at the Pacific Northwest Paranormal Conference. Her subject was to be the Urandir case. When word of the controversy began to spread like wildfire, the committee representing the conference cancelled her invitation and replaced her with Mr. Gevaerd from Brazil. The conference then initiated a comprehensive, independent investigation of the case. Their ultimate conclusion was that the case was a hoax of the worst possible caliber.

Next, Linda began talking about the scientific developments of the cases. She had submitted the bed sheet for scientific analysis and then quoted the results of this investigation on the "Coast to Coast" radio show with George Noorey. His purported listening audience is in the millions. Linda announced that the scientific analysis of the material demonstrated that the heat marking of the material defied explanation. Shortly following this, A.J. Gevaerd and the Brazilian research team found the gentleman who claimed to have made the mysterious marking—by using a torch with the material resting in a metal plate. It seems that he and other colleagues who were in Urandir's employ were not paid what was owed, resulting in bad feelings and a dispute. They were told to leave and complied with Urandir's wishes. However, the hard feeling generated made them quite vocal.

The information at this point began flowing at a rapid rate, especially through the Internet. Shortly after the confession of the Brazilian blowtorch eyewitness, there was a surprise appearance of the scientist who Linda quoted on the air. The scientist told the radio audience an entirely different story, criticized Linda for taking her report out of context, and rebuked her for only quoting the sections that made the case look favorable to her cause. This added even more flavor and controversy to the mystery of her involvement.

On the heels of all this uncertainty was the upcoming National MUFON Conference; they had invited Linda to speak and her topic was the Urandir case. The news of this traveled at break-neck speed to Brazil and to A. J. Gevaerd, who was not pleased since he was the official MUFON representative for his country. This generated more confusion and official arguments between the directors of the organization. Finally, in an effort to make peace, A. J. was invited to attend the conference but warned not to create a scene or make waves by open confrontation with Linda. When he heard this he took it as an insult and threatened to resign. Fortunately, this did not take place. Finally, A. J. was appeased with positive articles following the conference written in the *MUFON Journal*.

At the time of this writing, most of the excitement has settled and the case is not discussed, except in closed circles. I am still having the opinion that this was probably one of the most dangerous, notorious, and widespread hoaxes involving the subject of Ufology ever. I do not believe there will ever be a satisfactory explanation for the actions of Linda Moulton Howe. I also have great hopes that Urandir will be stopped before another infamous worldwide headline appears in the media.

Chapter 3

VARGINHA, BRAZIL
MY INVESTIGATION BEGINS

I first became aware of the Varginha, Brazil case shortly after it happened in 1996. Many of my close friends in Brazil who were UFO researchers were extremely excited about this UFO event, and their enthusiasm spread rapidly around the world.

Ordinarily the city of Varginha is certainly not one of those areas that would attract tourists, and especially not tourists from the United States.

Downtown Varginha

I have found that although there is a large amount of U.S. tourism in Brazil, the destination of most travelers are to the greater metropolitan cities such as Rio de Janerio, Brasilia, or Sao Paulo. There are also specific parts of the country that attract large numbers of tourists from Europe, and these same areas seem to be relatively unknown to the U.S. tourist industry. For example, there is a beautiful northeast coast city called Fortaleza where one can see miles and miles of sandy beaches and palm trees swaying in the natural ocean breezes. This paradise attracts travelers from Portugal and other European countries, but as far as the U.S. is concerned, it seems a closely guarded secret.

Almost everyone who travels to Brazil becomes aware of its secret treasured areas, such as on the southeastern tip of the country where the world's most beautiful falls can be found. The largest city in this region is Foz do Iguacu, which also happens to be a UFO hotspot. But the average traveler does not come to see UFOs; they are there to see the beauty of the falls and to embark upon the great rivers of the region.

In contrast to the tourist hot spots is Varginha, located in the state of Minas Gerais, northwest of Sao Paulo. It has a rich history, famous for its mining of gold and other important minerals. I would describe Varginha, even today, as a quiet community with a rapidly increasing population. It now stands at about 130,000 people and is known for its coffee and dairy production. The geography consists of rolling hills with green vegetation and sleepy little valleys. As in other parts of the country, the people are friendly and go out of their way to accommodate visitors. I found them proud of their heritage, hard working and sincere. The following are some modern statistics pertaining to Varginha:

Area: 396,39 km2
Postal Code: 37.100.000
Distance from the capital: 300 km
Geographic Region: Southern part of Minas Gerais state
Airports: 1
Bank Agencies: 14
Altitude: 950 mt
Students: 31.752
Urban Area: 95%
Auditoriums: 5
Libraries: 4
Oncology Centers: 1
Population: 277 habitantes / Km^2 (Pop / area)
Radio Stations: 5 (Melodia, FM; Transamerica, FM; Transamerica Light, AM; Vanguarda, FM; and Comunitária Princesa, FM)
TV Stations: EPTV (Rede Globo), Alterosa (SBT) e Princesa (Cultura)
First Degree Schools: 50
Second Degree Schools: 43
Life Expectation: 73.6 years
Heliports: 1
Hospitals: 3 (one, municipal)
Hotels: 18
Edited Journals: 9 (3 daily, 2 weekly, 4 periodical)

Hospital Beds: 324
Allotments and edifications: 36 mil
Microrregon: Low Sapucaí
Motels: 7
Museums: 1
Estimated inhabitants number: 120 mil habitantes
Spots of public illumination: 11.346
Female Population: 50.846 (1996)
Male Population: 49.322 (1996 - Total 100.168 habit.)
Health Posts: 17 (6 policlinics)
Principal economical activities: Industry; Commerce; Coffee Culture
Principal Product: coffee (the second commerce rank in the Country)
Main access road: BR-381 (Fernão Dias)
First Aid Stations: 2 (one, municipal)
Personal Income: R$ 4.005,39
Convention Rooms: 5
Theaters: 2
Cell Phones: 5.824 (97/98)
Telephones: 19.656 (97/98)
Cell Phone Towers: 4
Universities/faculties: 4 (16 courses)

Many times in the past I had visited Brazil and asked if it would be possible for me to go to Varginha and do a personal investigation of the UFO event of 1996. Each time I was discouraged by locals from doing so. Some of the reasons given were:
1. It is too dangerous to go there because the Brazilian military does not want visitors from the U.S. snooping around.
2. You won't see anything there because all the areas have either been built over or are walled off from public view.
3. All the people involved with the case will not talk with you because they have been intimidated by the military.
4. Most of the people involved have moved away.
5. You won't find any physical evidence because it has all be picked up or destroyed.

These were all reasons given to keep me away. The more this was done, the more intrigued I became. My trip to Brazil in 2002 was planned in advance. I was to present material at conferences in several different cities. I thought this to be a golden opportunity to get to Varginha and insisted it be included in my itinerary. Even at this stage of planning, I was again discouraged from going there because of rumors of difficulty with air transportation, increased expenses, inconvenient hours and airport problems. My comments about these problems amounted to, "I don't care how inconvenient this is going to be or what hours or lengths I have to fly. Just get me the necessary tickets!" With that, all problems seemed to magically disappear.

The planning for this trip to Brazil included a very dear friend of mine, Phil Serrins, who I have known for many years. We had been traveling companions on many jaunts about the world. His profession is an optometrist and his practice is in central California. Among his many talents is his ability to act as an amateur photographer; he was delighted when I asked him to not only become my traveling companion, but also use his talents to photograph the important portions of the trip with both video and still photography.

Our schedule allowed for a conference in the major city of Sao Paulo, and then on to the southernmost portion of our trip for an additional small conference in Foz do Iguacu. This left us time for some sightseeing and UFO investigation.

We had just returned to Sao Paulo from the southern area of Brazil and spent one night in a hotel. The next morning we caught our flight to Varginha. The trip was with a small but very popular and busy Brazilian airline. The aircraft was modern and clean, and the service was as good as one could expect from any of the major carriers. The flight was not a long one, taking about one and half-hours. As viewed from our aircraft window, this portion of the Brazilian countryside was vastly different from what I had seen in other parts of the country. It was more arid, with sparse vegetation that painted the rolling hills with varying shades of green.

I was so engrossed in gazing out of the window that I didn't notice how quickly the time had passed. Suddenly, I could feel the aircraft begin to descend. I craned my neck to see where the airport was located and had difficulty recognizing it. Since I was a licensed private pilot in the United States, I had some experience in locating airports from the altitude we were flying. Unfortunately, I did not observe the landing strip we were heading for. The aircraft made a few turns and steadied at a low altitude above the ground. It was our final approach and I was not expecting to see what was waiting ahead. To my surprise, instead of seeing the usual larger commercial aerodrome, what we were heading into was a single runway facility. I could not even make out the tower. I thought to myself, "Could this actually be our destination, Varginha?" At that moment I noticed Phil was already photographing our landing through his window. I remarked that we were evidently landing at a tiny rural facility. Soon we felt the jolt as the aircraft wheels touched the darkly paved runway. Phil was still pressed up against the window with camera rolling. As the aircraft slowed, I could make out what appeared to be a taxiway and a small building I assumed was the terminal. Sure enough, we turned toward the building and came to a slow stop. At that point the ground crew rolled out a set of metal steps in preparation for our arrival. Since the day was drawing to a close, the afternoon light was dimming and dusk was already upon us. Our seats were in the rear section of the aircraft and that meant we would be some of the last passengers to depart. I continued to look out the window and was shocked to see a small crowd coming from the terminal, heading directly to our airplane. I remarked to Phil that security must be quite lax at this facility. He smiled and laughed, saying, "I can certainly agree with that statement."

I also mentioned that these people did not seem to be departing with the passengers coming down the stairs, and wondered what in the world their purpose was for being there. We slowly approached the open doorway of the airplane. I felt the fresh air caress my cheeks. It felt very pleasant, as there was a refreshing smell indicative of a rural area without pollution. I was the first one out the doorway of the aircraft and onto the steps, and Phil was close behind me. I negotiated the last step and my feet touched the ground. I saw and felt a hand grasp mine and hear a friendly voice say,

Ubirajara ("Bira") Rodrigues, foremost Brazilian researcher into the events at Varginha.

"Dr. Leir, I am Rudolfo Rodrigues and this is my father Ubirajara. As you know, he was the major investigator involved with the ET case here. We would all like to welcome you to Varginha."

I was astonished, to say the least, but had no idea what was yet to transpire. It was only a matter of seconds before other outstretched hands reached for mine. Each person presented himself to us, speaking in Portuguese and others in English. The last person to greet us was none other than the mayor of Varginha. He spoke few words in English but his warm handshake expressed his feeling in a way that took no language to understand. I had a hard time grasping the reality of the situation. Was it really possible that all these kind folk had come to the airport to welcome me to their small city? I felt this was an honor and a moment I should not easily forget.

As the passengers from this flight filtered into the small terminal, the baggage handlers began placing the luggage on a mobile cart adjacent to the portable stairs. Rudolfo asked which luggage belonged to us. With that, each of the bystanders grabbed our bags with great gusto and began to carry them away. We followed the crowd and exited this small, rural airport on the way to the parking area.

When we arrived in the parking lot I thought I was really in a big city. It is almost impossible to describe the large amount of cars parked there in comparison to the perceived size of the airport facility. I had second thoughts about the amount of air traffic this facility could handle in a single day. Perhaps it was a much larger amount than I had originally thought. Ahead, I heard Rudolfo say we had arrived. There were a number of cars lined up and our baggage had been placed inside. I was to ride with Rudolfo and Bira; Phil was escorted into a second waiting vehicle. I inquired as to our destination and was told we were first going to be taken to our hotel where we could check in, freshen up, and then meet them later that evening for dinner.

Our vehicle navigated its way through numerous two-lane roads and then pulled out onto what appeared to be a freeway. We sped along at a rapid clip for almost a half hour. It was getting more difficult to visualize the countryside, as the night was closing in on us rapidly. What I did see was reminiscent of what we saw from the airplane window. The terrain was vastly different than what I had become accustomed to south of Sao Paolo. It consisted of rolling hills, sparsely covered in vegetation, and reminded me very much of the area in California where I had just come from. I saw an ever-increasing number of buildings and road signs, indicating our approach to the city. The amount of traffic began to increase, which was a sure sign that we were in an urban sprawl. After a few more stoplights and right and left turns we pulled into the parking lot of what appeared to be a restaurant. Two more cars, which were part of our entourage, parked close by. Soon, I heard Phil's familiar laugh and observed his exit from one of the parked vehicles.

We were escorted through the restaurant into the lobby of the adjacent hotel. It was a one story "L" shaped building with the lobby in the front. Once the formalities of the check-in procedure were completed, we were escorted to our room with a plan to meet in the restaurant later.

It didn't take Phil long to remark that it was the end of the day and he would certainly enjoy a beer. Our room had a small refrigerator, so I pulled open the door and read the list of contents to my companion; the menu was in Portuguese but still translatable. He decided to sample one of the unknown Brazilian beers and I settled for a Guarana drink, which had become one of my favorites in Brazil.

After a test of our camera equipment we decided to explore our surroundings. The small hotel was similar to one of the standard motels in the U.S. I found there was a great difference in the meaning of the use of the word hotel and motel in Brazil. It seems the latter is a place to bring your girlfriend or a place to acquire a girl for a romantic evening, whereas the term hotel was reserved for more ordinary traveling. Phil and I strolled through the plush gardens and spotted a pool in the rear portion of the property. Since it never really gets cold in Brazil by North American standards, one can take advantage of the swimming facilities at almost anytime. I inquired of my companion as to whether he was considering a swim and was told in no uncertain terms the consumption of a couple of more beverages such as the one he was drinking was as close as he was prepared to come to liquid at the moment. We returned to our room, flipped on the television and were amazed to get CNN in English. After a quick shower we hustled off to our rendezvous with Rudolfo and Bira.

Phil and I were first to arrive in the small adjoining restaurant. Since this was off the path of normal Brazilian tourism, it became a bit difficult to make our needs understood without being able to speak Portuguese. I have come to learn that we all as human beings posses the skills to go beyond the language barrier to accomplish understanding. Fortunately, this was one of the times when this rule came into play. We were shown to a nice table and only a short time passed before I heard Bira's voice. He was with his son Rudolfo again, and with them was a third person who I recognized from one of my previous visits to Brazil. Nelson turned and gave me a warm embrace. I in turn introduced him to Phil. We all sat and took part in our first feast in Varginha.

After dinner the tone became more serious as plans were drawn for the coming days. One of my concerns was that I would be able to investigate the case in my own fashion, looking for essentials in my field of interest. I explained all I had previously heard about the case and where my primary fields of interest were. I also, without hesitation, brought forth the numerous rumors I had heard pertaining to the inaccessibility of witnesses, as well as stories about the growth of the area and obstruction of those geographical points I was interested in seeing. I told the group that my intentions were not exactly the same as some of the previous American investigators, as my primary area of interest was physical evidence and any relationships to the worldwide abduction phenomena. My trepidations were soon put to rest as Bira explained through his son that although building projects now obscured some of the sites, there were still many ways that they could be viewed and photographed. In reference to the witnesses, he told us that he and his staff would do everything they could to make them available to us for interviews on camera. The plan for tomorrow was to meet here at the hotel in the AM and then proceed to Bira's Institute of Ufological Research, where I would be given a tour and start our day. With this agreed upon, we all adjourned for the evening.

Phil, who was, as usual, the first out of bed in the morning, popped out of the shower and before I had a chance to place my feet on the cold tile floor he announced he was going out for coffee. This came as no surprise, as this was his habit over the many years we have known each other, and his custom when traveling. I told him I'd meet him in the restaurant.

The weather outside was warm and sunny with a light gentle breeze. I made my way to the restaurant and found Phil sitting at one of the large tables. He had brought some of the camera equipment with him and was fussing with his new digital still camera while slowly sipping his coffee. He smiled and said, "Well it's about time you decided to come out. I already had coffee and breakfast, and by the way, I was outside already filming the rear portion of the hotel." I knew Phil's habits quite well and only took part of his statement as the truth. I knew he had not had breakfast since he had no knowledge of the language and could not make himself understood. I told him since he had already eaten, I was sure he would not mind if I had some breakfast also. With that I looked into the adjoining anteroom and noticed a table set with delicious looking fruits, breads, cereals, cheeses and other enticing forms of breakfast repast. In addition, there was coffee, tea, and a host of other condiments. I told Phil I would be right back and proceeded toward this area of food delicacies. A waiter spied my interest and waved me toward the food. As we approached the table he reached over and handed me a plate and cloth napkin. I thanked him in the traditional language by saying, "Obrigado!" and proceeded to fill my plate with the food at hand. With a cup of tea in one hand and the filled plate in the other, I preceded back into the eating area where Phil stood with a shocked look on his face. "Where did you get all that?" he asked. "Oh, it's right there in the other room, but what difference does it make since you have already eaten?" I asked, smiling from ear to ear. Phil laughed and headed for the table, returning in a few moments with a fresh cup of coffee and a plate piled high with food. We sat, had a good laugh and began our meal.

It was only a few minutes later when we heard familiar voices. Bira and Rudolfo had just arrived. We greeted them with open hugs. Since they were already familiar with the hotel and its breakfast procedures, they took turns in gathering their food. The waiter arrived shortly after and a brief conversation in Portuguese took place with little understanding on my part. Soon it was down to business. We were to leave the hotel and head for Ubirajara's

Institute for Ufolological Research where we would be filled in on the entire Varginha case.

Brazil Aliens Hit Front Page of Wall Street Journal

I have mentioned previously that this case received worldwide attention and surprised many of us here in the United States engaged in UFO research because of an article which appeared in the conservative Wall Street Journal newspaper. Finally, it seems, the U.S. mainstream press has noticed that Brazil, one of the world's largest countries, is in a total uproar over the claim that its military may have captured two or more alien creatures. Though the following story from the prestigious Wall Street Journal has a tongue-in-cheek tone bordering on derision, it does not entirely dismiss the possibility that something remarkable may have happened in Brazil. For balance, see also the statement from British researcher Graham Birdsall, later in the book. CNI News thanks Patricia Welch for forwarding this story, which has been republished around the world and is available on numerous web sites even today. The following is a reprint of the original article obtained from an Internet site:

Tale of Stinky Extraterrestrials Stirs Up UFO Crowd in Brazil
by Matt Moffett
Staff Reporter, Wall Street Journal
July 12, 1996

VARGINHA, Brazil -- The incident that made this town a hot spot in the intergalactic search for intelligent life started quite innocently. On a Saturday afternoon stroll in January, a trio of young women decided to take a shortcut home through a vacant lot. In a clump of weeds, the three said, they encountered a creature like nothing they had seen before.

"It wasn't a man or an animal—it was something different," said one of the women, Katia Andrade. The being had oily brown skin and rubbery limbs, she said. Three rounded protrusions sprouted from its oversized head. Standing out in a different way was the creature's odor: One ghastly whiff weakened the knees. As for the stranger's demeanor, the women unanimously, if tactlessly, agreed: It was "muddle-headed." When the creature wagged its big noggin dizzily in their direction, the three women ran off.

Word of this encounter, spreading rapidly through the coffee bars where Varginha's 120,000 inhabitants trade gossip, would soon meld in the public imagination with other unusual occurrences: sightings of a strange cigar-shaped flying object, a mustering of troops and vehicles at a nearby infantry base and a peculiar bustle at the municipal hospital. Goaded by self-styled UFO savants and a ravenous national media, residents rather matter-of-factly embraced a stupefying conclusion: Several aliens from a wayward space ship had been captured and brutalized by troops from the Brazilian army.

Creature Feature

Bristling denials from the military, which once compiled a lengthy record of abuses against the terrestrial population, have only served to inflame public suspicion. The upshot: The army and the now-famous space aliens find themselves locked in a pitched battle for the hearts and minds of this provincial community. Doltish and malodorous though these space celebrities might be, mere men in uniform are proving no match for the first creatures of any kind from Varginha to land on a national magazine cover.

"For extraterrestrials they may not be much, but they are the biggest thing we've ever had in Varginha," says a young woman named Nilda, scanning the nighttime sky from a downtown park bench. Had the armed forces not interfered, she says, locals might have scrubbed the visitors, taught them the language... in sum... made something of them. "But they never had a chance," Nilda says with a sigh. Her anger at the military's alleged inhospitality sparked a tiff with her boyfriend, a private in the infantry.

Mystic Point

The army finds itself besieged on several fronts. A local mystic predicts that Varginha will suffer some kind of cataclysm this September as retribution for its blitzkrieg on the interplanetary visitors. An armed-forces news conference marking "Victory Day" in World War II degenerated into a shouting match between a general and a television reporter pressing him about the extraterrestrials. An official briefing to debunk UFO conspiracies was overshadowed by an auto mechanic's claim to have seen yet another weird cylindrical aircraft, a cosmic encounter he re-enacted with the aid of an aluminum coffee thermos.

To some extent the army is paying for past sins. During an oppressive 20-year dictatorship ending in 1985, the Brazilian military eliminated any number of earthbound political enemies by "disappearing" them. If the army was capable of liquidating human beings without a trace, locals ask, why couldn't it carry such a "dirty war" to outer space?

In truth, the current, cash-strapped incarnation of Brazil's army poses little threat to anyone, least of all an enemy that might have ray guns. In some training exercises Brazilian troops have been reduced to pointing their rifles and shouting "bang" in order to save ammo.

At the army base near Varginha, an inquiry concerning the extra-terrestrials is received warily by a private, who turns it over to a sergeant, who then passes it along a major. From there the matter is sent back down to another sergeant, who hands the question over to Capt. Eduardo Calza, the outfit's sad-sack spokesman. "You know, I used to get calls about the base talent show," he says.

The Official Explanation

Capt. Calza says he can't vouch for what the three women saw in January. But the activity on the base that fateful weekend, he insists, was anything but otherworldly: New inductees to a sergeants' training school went on parade and a truck convoy was driven to the repair shop. Concurrently, at the town hospital, trucks delivered new cardio-vascular equipment and an ambulance dropped off an exhumed corpse—a human body, officials insist.

"Sure, tell us another story," says Vitorio Pacaccini, the bearded, effusive UFO investigator at the eye of the Varginha storm. Based upon interviews with supposed eyewitnesses, Mr. Pacaccini has pieced together what he considers to be a more plausible reconstruction of January's events: A small alien craft on an unknown mission over Varginha crashed near the city limits, sending its crew of smelly, spaced-out extraterrestrials ambling about the town. Subsequently, Mr. Pacaccini maintains, military death squads in camouflage fatigues hunted down the visitors, poked and prodded the corpses at the municipal hospital, and then shipped them off to parts unknown. "It's very straightforward," he says.

Mr. Pacaccini's brand of hucksterism is characteristic of the frontier atmosphere in a town where the architecture is of the Quonset-hut school and the newspaper is staffed by a lone reporter. Since the initial sighting, Mr. Pacaccini, a longtime UFO buff, has essentially abandoned his job as a business consultant to provide one-stop shopping for visiting journalists.

To date, Brazil's leading television magazine has done three programs here. A two-hour nationally televised documentary on Varginha pulled in so many viewers on a recent Saturday night that it was repeated in its entirety the following weekend. Two of the women who made the initial sighting now demand $200 for each interview.

Alien Playground

With an eye toward promoting Varginha, city fathers are thinking of building a park in the creature's honor. Deputy Mayor Paulo Vitor Freire says: "We would never have imagined that so many international organizations take interest in cases like ours."

Yes Varginha, there is a support group known as Abductees Anonymous and a research organization called Operation Right to Know. Stanton Friedman, a Canada-based UFO expert, says Varginha has the makings of a "cosmic Watergate."

If anything, the case may be suffering from eyewitness overkill. By now there have been so many sightings of the creature—seven at last count—that it is unclear how all of these beings could have fit into the minivan-sized spacecraft that was spotted here in January. "Lots of us get into cars with five or six other passengers in them," Mr. Pacaccini retorts, drawing a down-to-earth analogy. True, but usually on short trips; seldom when driving to another galaxy.

Mr. Pacaccini's most tantalizing proofs are videotaped statements by two young men in civilian clothes that claim to be members of the military detail that disposed of the alien visitors. It is impossible to determine the tapes' authenticity, however, since Mr. Pacaccini won't reveal the men's names. He says they fear reprisals.

There is also a troubling lack of physical evidence, unless you count descriptions of a paw print seen by one witness. The print is said to resemble what a human hand would look like with the palm flat, and a space opened up between the ring and pinky fingers and the other three digits. Fans of the old Star Trek series may sense a stirring of recognition. It looks remarkably like Mr. Spock's Vulcan salute.

Chapter 4

THE VARGINHA CASE UNFOLDS

EVENT # 1

I have been asked many times to make a comparison between the 1996 Varginha, Brazil case to the United States, Roswell event which occurred in 1947. In my opinion, the cases closely resemble each other, but there are also many significant differences. First and foremost, the Roswell case centers on the testimony of a *large* group of witnesses to the crash of an unusual saucer-like vehicle. In addition, there are a much smaller number who are able to recall alien bodies strewn about the crash sight. In the Varginha case, only a *small* number of witnesses are available who can describe the crash landing of a cylindrical craft. Most of the witnesses from Varginha described not a crash or its debris, but what they believed were alien creatures interacting with the Brazilian military and civilian population. The next most significant comparative factor is the time element; with about 50 years difference between each case. The witnesses to the Roswell incident are rapidly dying off which is in distinct contradiction to what is happening in Varginha. More new witnesses seem to be making themselves available for interviews as the months and years go by. There is also a great difference between the intrinsic populations of Roswell and Varginha. Although it would appear that both groups were severely repressed by the military establishment, the Brazilians appear to be far more prone to gossip and cause the rapid spread of information amongst the locals. I believe this has resulted in the large amount of unsubstantiated stories revolving around the case. I personally consider the Varginha case to be "the modern Roswell".

The Beginning
Phil and I rushed to our room to pick up our necessities, including our camera equipment, then headed directly to the parking lot where we rendezvoused with Bira and Rudolfo, who were waiting patiently by their car. We jumped in and began our first sightseeing trek through the streets of Varginha. I inquired as to the length of time it would take to reach Bira's Institute and was told about 10 or 15 minutes. This was the first time we were able to see what the city itself looked like, as our trip to the hotel from the

airport was during the nighttime. The buildings were mainly one story and looked similar to other parts of Brazil I had previously seen. It also reminded me of areas in Southern California where I lived. The streets were slightly narrow by American standards and most had sidewalks. The weather was pleasant, sunny and warm. Time passed quickly as Rudolfo pointed out some of the interesting sites and told us what parts of the city we were going through. We made numerous turns and finally slowed to a stop in front of an iron gate. A small sign on the adjoining pillar stated: "Institute For Ufological Research". Leading the way, Bira swung the iron gate open and welcomed us inside. As we entered the building, I realized this was not just an educational center, but also an ornate living quarters. As we entered what appeared to be a small living room, we heard a female voice calling to Bira. There was a brief vocal exchange in Portuguese between Bira and a young lady who was introduced to us as Bira's girlfriend. She warmly greeted both Phil and I and offered us refreshments. I followed along as Rudolfo gestured to us to accompany he and his father through a series of small halls and doorways. We then entered an office that was adorned with numerous filing cabinets lining the walls On one wall of the room there was a desk, meticulously arranged, and a computer. This was Bira's office and the filing cabinets contained the results of his UFO investigations. He had been investigating the phenomena in Brazil for some 36 years. The filing cabinets along one solid wall contained all the material on the Varginha case. These files consisted of testimony, drawings, photographs and other data pertaining to his investigation. Another adjoining room was a library filled with books referencing the UFO subject. On the walls were numerous photographs, maps and articles written in Portuguese—all pertaining to UFOs. Next we entered a room large enough to seat approximately 50 persons, complete with chairs arranged in theater fashion. In the front of the room was a large television set, a podium, and an elongated table. I asked Rudolfo if this was used for lectures and he nodded back yes. This would be a great place to set up the camera for interviews and I voiced my opinion to the group. All agreed, and kindly offered the room for whatever we wished.

Since the opportunity existed, I suggested the first to be interviewed would be Ubirajara himself. I would open my investigation of the case by a general review from the "horse's mouth". Since he was the initial investigator of the case, I considered him to be the leading authority. We all agreed. Phil, Rodolpho and I set up the camera equipment and placed three chairs in the front of the room. I would sit in the middle so I could move the microphone between the person I was interviewing and the interpreter.

Left to right: Phil Serrins, Dr. Leir and Ubirajara.

Bira would be to my right and Rudolfo would sit on the left so he could do the interpretation for the camera. Bira's girlfriend, Beca, was kind enough to set up a table with refreshments, so after a quick meal we started the interview.

I began with a brief statement on who I was and what my mission was in Brazil. I introduced both Ubirajara and Rudolfo. My first query to Bira was having him explain the Varginha case in his own words. Bira began by telling us the case was far more complex than one might imagine. He went on to explain that time had passed since the days of the actual event, and rumors had begun to circulate both in and out of his country. Some of them had a basis in truth and others did not. I told him one of my endeavors was to sift out the rumors from the actual facts of the case and, if possible, document their authenticity with physical evidence. He explained the case was not just comprised of one event, but rather a series of events which were probably related.

Ubirajara started by telling us there was even confusion as to the original date of the event because of conflicting testimony of the eyewitnesses. The accepted date now is January 20, 1996. He was not present on the original date because he was out of town due to business and did not return until January 21st. He arrived home at approximately 10:30 AM and immediately began to receive telephone calls in reference to the case. One was from a shopkeeper who told him about a girl who had seen a strange creature or monster. Bira found out there was more than one girl involved in the incident and that they lived at Tapaj Us Street with their mother, Luisa. Bira questioned a shopkeeper close to that area and she told him that large numbers of people were exploring and walking around the area involved. The lady happened to be a friend of the girl's mother and explained that the girls arrived home that afternoon screaming, crying and completely terrified. They had seen something very ugly.

Bira told us that it was only a few days following this testimony when another famous UFO investigator in Brazil by the name of Vitorio Pacaccini joined him in the investigation. He then explained that the most important event took place at 3:30 PM on the afternoon of the 20th. This was the event that he originally heard about and had involved the same three young girls described by the shopkeeper.

These three young women were walking home from work by taking a short cut through a vacant lot when they encountered a strange looking humanoid creature crouching by a concrete block wall. Their first impression was that the creature appeared to be hurt and suffering pain. The three girls, Liliane Fatima Silva, 16 years of age, her sister Valquira Fatima Silva, 14 years old, and a friend, Katia Andrade Xavier, 22 years old, were terrified of the creature they had just seen.

Eyewitness sketch of kneeling alien being.

Thinking it was the devil, they turned and ran to their homes—approximately one and a third kilometers away. The two sisters ran into their house and directly into the outstretched arms of their mother, Luiza. Bira was really impressed with the girl's testimony and especially that of Liliane, who burst into tears during the interview. He also stated that Katia was also in tears during her interview.

Drawing made by eyewitness
of alien being.

They described the creature as follows: It stood about four to five feet tall with dark brown, oily, greasy skin. It had a short neck with a large head showing no hair at all. The head contained two large red eyes that were slightly upturned at the outer ends. The eyes did not show a pupil. It had a very small mouth and nose, as well as three protuberances on the top of its head going from front to back. These were suggestive of horns and are what gave the girls the impression that this was the devil. Katia, who works as a maid and has three children of her own, described the creature as being stupefied, and stated that it did not make any noise.

Bira requested to be taken to the exact spot where this occurred. The girls agreed and he personally was able to investigate the area where the creature was kneeling. He was mystified when he noticed a strange round narrow hole in the ground, about the size of a large pen, at the area where the creature had been crouching. Since there was some inclement weather that had occurred after the event, additional evidence was not obtained such as footprints or earth markings.

My search of the literature concerning this case reports the following episode, pertaining to the mother of the two girls who were sisters, Luiza Helena Fatima de Silva. It states she saw the alien creature in Jardim Andere district on January the 20th and reported a peculiar smell when she went to the park at 4:00 PM. I personally questioned Mrs. Silva in reference to this statement and she denied it. I believe this is an important issue, as the rumors of strange smells have become associated with this case. I questioned Bira about this story and he told us the case was filled with rumors, which totally disregarded the facts.

Another rumor has it that Mrs. Silva reported four Brazilian men, wearing white and cream-colored Armani suits, who visited her. The men supposedly offered her a large sum of money to say that her daughters lied about seeing the alien creature. They reportedly showed up at her home when her husband, a bus driver, was at work. They also told her they would return and pay her in cash. It has also been reported that they drove a navy blue 1994 Lincoln Continental with a Distrito Federal (Brasalia) license plate. I an currently unable to determine if this statement has a basis in fact.

Interview with Liliane and Valquria

It is time to share with you the on-camera interview with two of the girls Ubirajara had talked about, Liliane and Valquiria. We will pick up the interview with Ubirjara again in chapter five. He had not only granted me an interview with him on camera, but also was kind enough to make arrangements for me to directly interview some of the eyewitnesses, including the girls. The first of these interviews was arranged for the second day of our visit. We were taken directly to the Silva home where we were able to talk with not only two of the girls, Liliane and Valquiria, but also their mother, Luiza Helena. Unfortunately, Katia had moved out of the area and was not going to be available. I inquired if the family was still in touch with Katia and they told me they were, but had not heard from her in some time.

On our way to the house we drove through the narrow streets of a densely populated, single story housing area. It was not one of the most prosperous neighborhoods of Varginha; as in other areas we had seen, the streets were clean, free from litter, and the walls showed no graffiti. The farther we drove, the more meager the surroundings became. Although the apparent cleanliness continued, there were signs of poverty, which were becoming more noticeable. Front yards that were decorated with plants and vines were now naked and showed signs that the earth had not been cultivated for a long time. The housing in previous areas showed paint that had clearly been applied in the near past. Now it had degenerated to cracked and peeling specimens, patched with stucco and other such substitute materials. Soon we pulled to the curb in front of small stucco-finished home, surrounded by a block wall which concealed a modest courtyard entryway. The area was covered with green lush foliage. We exited the automobile, carrying our camera equipment. A couple of house cats scooted by in front of us as we approached the door. The front door was open, but the entryway was obscured by a metal screen door. Startled, I heard a loud shrill shriek coming from one of the bushes. Both Phil and I flinched at the sound and turned to see what was making it. There, standing formidably on a branch of one of the bushes, was a large very colorful blue and yellow parrot. He turned his head and let out another loud shriek. We all laughed. Bira knocked on the screen and soon we were greeted by a short, stocky, dark-haired lady who seemed in her late fifty's. Some words were exchanged in Portuguese and we were ushered inside. Once inside Rudolfo introduced us to Luiza, mother of Liliane and Valquiria. She in turn introduced us to the girls. The room was a small living room, approximately eight by ten feet. It had simple furnishings, which seem to fit nicely into their Brazilian-style surroundings. The walls were adorned with numerous decorations consisting of religious symbols and photos of family members. Bira and Rudolfo explained to our hosts what my mission was in Varginha. They were told I wanted to do a short interview on camera with each of them separately. I felt it was of the utmost importance to have each of the individuals involved in the case interviewed in this manner so they would not influence each other's stories.

Phil and I mutually agreed on the placement of the camera, and determined the best angles and lighting for the interviews. We decided not to use individual microphones, as the room was small and the sound was satisfactory as heard through the camera. This decision, we found later, was a mistake, as we had not anticipated the sound effects of our friend the parrot shrieking through all the interviews. Two chairs were placed at one end of the room. Rudolfo would remain near the camera and do his interpretation from that position; he wouldn't be filmed and only his voice would be heard. One of the factors we could not control was the temperature in the room. The front door had to be left open, as there was no air-conditioning. This presented a complicating factor, as we could not control the sounds coming in through the open door. This, of course, included the shrieking squawk of the parrot.

The first to be interviewed was Valquiria. She seemed slightly nervous so I kept my opening remarks subdued in an attempt to set the pace for the interview. I will be referenced as Dr. L, and Valquiria will be Val. The interview went as follows:

Interview with Valquiria

Dr. L: Valquiria, I want to thank you very much for allowing me to interview you today. Please sit back and relax. My questions will be simple and easy for you to answer. How well do remember the events of that very special day in January, 1996?

Val.: Oh, I remember them very well, just as if they happened yesterday.

Dr. L: Good, I am glad to hear that. Can you tell us what happened on that day?

Val.: Yes. The three of us, Katia, Liliane and myself were on our way home from work. We had decided to take a shortcut. We were getting close to home when up ahead we saw a very strange sight. There was some sort of a creature in a crouched position by a wall, up ahead and to our left. First we thought it was some young kid but as we got closer we got a better look and realized it was not a kid or an animal. We all saw the creature at about the same time. Liliane screamed and we all turned and ran for home.

Dr. L: Can you describe what you saw?

Val.: It was a short creature and it was in a kneeling position with its head turned toward the wall. It was not moving, just crouching there.

Dr. L: What did the creature look like?

Val.: I did not see it for a very long period of time because I was so frightened I also turned and ran away. It was horrible looking, brown in color with an oily skin and a large head. It had what looked like a set of veins bulging out of the skin on the shoulders and on the neck. It had three bumps on the top of its head.

Dr. L: Did you see its eyes?

Val: I only saw a glimpse of them. It turned its head towards us just as I starting to run away. Its eyes were large and red in color. Its head looked too big for its body.

Dr. L: Did you all run away together or was it just you that ran first?

Val: We all ran away together but I might have been the first. Liliane and Katia were behind me.

Dr. L: Were you the only ones at that time who saw the creature or were there other people there also?

Val: No. It was only we.

Dr. L: Were there other people on the street at that time?

Val: The street was empty. We were the only ones there.

Dr. L: Did you notice if there was any smell when you arrived at the site where the creature was kneeling?

Val: No. There was no smell.

Dr. L: Are you absolutely sure? I am asking this because there are many rumors about this case and some of the witnesses have claimed there was a foul odor.

Val: I am absolutely sure there was no smell whatsoever.

Dr. L: Since you live in this area, you probably have seen lots of animals from the surrounding jungle areas. Did this look like an animal to you?

Val: No. This was not an animal.

Dr. L: What did you do when you all arrived home?

Val: We were very frightened and we told our mother.

Dr. L: What did she do, if anything?

Val: There was another lady there, our neighbor, and she took my mother back to the spot where we had seen the creature.

Dr. L: Did she also see the creature?

Val: No. It was gone when she arrived there. She only was able to see the footprints in the ground and the place where the tall grass had been pushed down where the creature had been kneeling by the wall.

Dr. L: She saw footprints?

Val: She saw them and told Ubirajara about them. I don't remember what she said they looked like.

Dr. L: Okay, Valquiria, I am going to switch gears for a moment and talk about some other things. Okay?

Val: Yes. Go ahead.

Dr. L: At anytime after this event happened, did you have any strange dreams?

Val: Um, well I don't know. Maybe one. It was about three months after this all happened. I dreamed I was flying and seeing stars and planets and stuff. It was really weird and I felt rotten when I got up in the morning. I must have gotten a cold or something. I just felt rotten. My mother remembers it well because Liliane also didn't feel so good. Maybe it was something we had eaten or the flu. I don't know.

Dr. L: Do you like salty foods? And by the way, when you go to the dentist how much injected anesthesia does it take to numb the area where he is going to work on your tooth?

Val: No. I really don't care for salty foods and it just usually takes one shot and everything seems to be numb.

At this point, my inquiry had referenced a few questions that are designed to indicate if the individual might be a subject of the abduction phenomena. Valquiria answered about 90% of these as a non-abductee. The one thing I found interesting at the time was her description of the dream she had three months following her episode. I had no way of knowing just how interesting this would become later.

Interview with Liliane

I thanked Valquiria for the time she spent with me. Next, ready and waiting was her sister, Liliane. She took the seat next to me. I told her I would be asking questions that were probably similar to some of the questions I had asked her sister. In reproducing Liliane's interview I will not repeat some of the same questions posed to her sister. Please assume the answers were the same or similar.

Dr. L: Thank you for allowing me the honor and privilege of letting me ask you some questions relative to the incident that occurred back in January of 1996. I will try and make the questions as easy as possible. Please just sit back and relax and answer them as honestly as you can. The first question I want to ask you are: Were you present with your sister Valquiria and your friend Katia when you saw the creature on that day?

Lil: Yes. I was there. We were all walking together through this passageway on the way home from work.

Dr. L: Can you tell us about what you saw?

Lil: We all saw a very strange looking creature kneeling close to a wall. When I first saw it I was terrified and thought it was the Devil. It had what looked like Devil horns on the top of its head. Three large bumps on the top of the head. No hair. Its skin was brown and shiny. It looked oily and there were some weird looking veins sticking out of the skin on the neck and shoulders. I was so frightened; I let out a loud scream. I think that also frightened my two friends. We all turned to run back home.

Dr. L: Did you notice any odor at the time you were there looking at the creature?

Lil: No. There was no smell at all.

Dr. L: Did you all run back together or one at a time?

The three girls who saw the kneeling alien creature point to the spot. Left to right: Katia, Liliane and Valquiria.

Dr. L: What happened that made you stay longer?

Lil: When we first arrived at the spot the creature was just kneeling there, very still and had its head turned towards the wall, but just before I turned to run home it turned its head and looked straight at me with its big red eyes. I felt sorry for it. I thought there must be something wrong with it. I don't know. It was just a feeling. Maybe it reacted to my scream. It was just weird. I don't know. I was very upset and frightened.

Dr. L: You mentioned to me before we started this interview that you had the impression that this was an intelligent creature. Can you explain?

Lil: No. I just know it was intelligent. I don't know why I felt that way. You know how sometimes when you see an animal like a cow and think how dumb it must be? Also when you have a pet like a dog and the dog seems to know exactly everything that you want him to do. This creature seemed to have high intelligence just like a human being.

Dr. L: Let's suppose there was a monkey, chimpanzee or ape sitting there. Would you consider them intelligent creatures?

Lil: No. They are different. They are animals.
Dr. L: Did you think this creature was not an animal?

Lil: That's right. It was not an animal.

Dr. L: Have you seen lots of animals from the wild since you have been living here?

Lil: Oh, yes. Many different kinds like snakes, birds, crocodiles, monkeys and all sorts of different ones.

Dr. L: Are you certain this was not some animal that you have never seen before?

Lil: No. It was not an animal. It was an intelligent creature.

Dr. L: When you arrived home did you, your sister or friend feel ill? Did you have any symptoms of headache, nausea, skin rash, or excessive thirst?

Lil: No. We all felt fine. We were all just very upset and crying.

Dr. L: Okay, what happened next after you arrived home?

Lil: We told our mother what happened and she ran to a neighbor's. They both went back to the spot together.

Dr. L: Was the creature still there when your mother arrived back at the spot?

Lil. No. She told us there was nothing there but footprints in the soft, long grass where it had been kneeling.
Dr. L: Okay. Liliane, I'm going to ask you some questions pertaining to other subjects.

At that point I switched my questions back to the abduction phenomena but in a way the witness would have no idea what answers I was searching for. Her testimony in this regard was pretty much the same as her sister's. The strange part came last and is as follows:

Dr. L: Liliane, did you at any point have any strange dreams following this incident?

Lil: Well, there is one I can think of that happened about three months later. I dreamed the creature was in my room and I wasn't afraid. That was all. I don't remember the rest.

I thanked Liliane for her time and wished her luck with all her future endeavors. The last person to interview in this group was Luiza Helena, the girl's mother.

Interview with Luiza Helena

I began the interview with Luiza Helena by telling her how honored I was to have the opportunity to interview she and her daughters. I explained I would not take a long time or ask her numerous questions that she has probably been asked a million times previously.

Dr. L: Luiza, how did you feel knowing your daughters may have seen a being from another world?

Luiza: I really did not know if this was one of God's creatures or something else. They were so terrified at what they saw.

Dr. L: Did you consider that this might have been one of God's creatures from another world?

Luiza: Yes, I did and in fact I felt that if it was truly one of God's creations from elsewhere, my daughters might have been chosen to have this experience. Before this actually happened, I felt something inside indicating we were going to have a strange and unusual experience. I believe it was God's will for this to happen. It was destiny.

Dr. L: Luiza, after your daughters came home and told you they had seen this strange creature, did you immediately go to the sight where this took place?

Luiza: Yes, I did. One of my neighbors came over and was quite concerned. She volunteered to go back with me.

Dr. L: What did you see when you got there?

Luiza: We went to the site where this creature was kneeling by a wall. The small field was empty. There was no sign of anything there, however the grass was smashed down at the spot where the girls said they saw it kneeling. It looked like there may have been imprints in the soft ground. I really didn't pay too much attention to them.

Dr. L: Is there anything further you can tell me about what happened that day?

Luiza: No, I really think you have heard it all by now.

Dr. L: Luiza, did you ever see a UFO or have an unusual experience you couldn't explain?

Luiza: When I was eight or nine years of age I was staying at my grandmother's house. I looked up on the hill out the front door and saw a very unusual small figure wearing strange clothing. Its head was covered with a hood. After that I saw these same figures many times. More than one, all dressed the same. We didn't want to talk about it. Some times I saw strange lights in the sky.

Dr. L: Did you ever have any lifelike dreams that involved flying machines or strange beings?

Luiza, at this point, stared straight ahead and there was a moment of complete silence before answering the question.

Luiza: I never told anybody about this but just after what happened to my daughters I had a dream that my daughters and I were sucked up out of the roof of our house into an airplane. I was terrified and don't remember much else about it.

Dr. L: Did you ever wake up in the morning with any strange marks on your body that you could not account for and weren't there when you went to bed?

Luiza: No, I don't think so.

Dr. L: Do you like to eat food with a lot of salt?

Luiza: Oh yes, I just love to pile on the salt on all foods I eat. I just can't get enough salt.

Dr. L: How is your vision at nighttime, in comparison to the way you see during the day?

Luiza: I only am able to see out of my left eye. I had a blood clot and have lost the vision in my other eye. I really don't notice the difference between my night and day vision.

Dr. L: Luiza, when you wear jewelry, do you notice if your skin turns color or if there is any other affect you have noticed?

Luiza: I can't wear jewelry at all because my arm or other parts start to turn numb. I have not noticed if there is any change in color.

Dr. L: Do you have any problems with electrical or electronic equipment?

Luiza: Sometimes when I walk into a room the lights will just go off or I will turn on a switch and nothing happens at all. Sometimes the TV will just change channels when I come into the room. It really makes me mad.

Dr. L: Have you ever had a dream where somebody was putting something inside your body?

Luiza: No.

Dr. L: After this event happened with your girls, did you remember if any one of you became ill?

Luiza: Yes, both Liliane and I got sick with some sort of a cold or something. It was hard to get rid of but finally went away. Valquiria didn't get sick at all.

Dr. L: Do you remember or do you know if Katia or anyone in her family became ill?

Luiza: No, I really don't know. We never talked about it.

Dr. L: Luiza, is there anything else you would like to tell me about?

Luiza: The only thing I can say is that this event has marked our lives forever.

I thanked Luiza for the time she gave to me and for the kindness she exhibited in honestly answering my questions.

Discussion

Since numerous investigators from Brazil and the United States had interviewed both of the girls and mother previously, I felt it would serve no purpose to quiz them again with the same type of questions they had previously been asked. Also for the sake of brevity, at this writing, I did not include all the questions asked during the interviews. I was interested mainly in three aspects of the event:

Their interaction with the event itself.

Their possible relationship to the abduction phenomena.

Their involvement with obtainable physical evidence.

It was interesting to learn that although the girls basically arrived on the scene at the same time, their individual feelings and reactions were somewhat different. It was only Liliane who seemed to find an emotional bond with the creature. The turning point, undoubtedly for her, was when the being turned its head and looked straight at her. It seemed at this point that she decided that this was not an animal, but an intelligent creature that apparently bonded with her emotionally. This reaction was slightly different than that of her sister Valquiria, who stated she felt instant terror, but in retrospect was able to set this feeling aside and also render an opinion that this was indeed an intelligent creature. The description of the creature was consistent by each of the girls. The mother, Luiza, on the other hand, had no direct contact with the being but still felt an emotional bond with the event that happened to her daughters.

The interview I conducted contained questions designed by our group, A&S Research, to rule either in or out the possibility of involvement with the alien abduction phenomena. Both of the girls responded with answers indicating a negative involvement, however the mother answered many of the questions in a positive manner. Most startling was her dream following the incident in which both she and her daughters were floating or " being sucked" out of the roof of their home into a waiting airplane. I did not pursue the description of the flying craft at this interview for two primary reasons. The first is that I did not want to suggest to this women that she might have been abducted with her two daughters. I felt this could be pursued at a later date. The other reason was solely due to time constraints; I had given her my word that the interview would be short and did not want to lose her confidence. Additional information indicating involvement in the phenomena was her description of the small hooded beings she had seen as a child. She also had told me (off camera) of other close relatives who had seen lights in the sky, had dreams of floating out of their houses into some kind of flying craft, and had marks on their bodies, etc. I had come to the conclusion that the mother and her family had a high probability of involvement with the abduction phenomenon.

One of the significant factors gleaned from the mother was her recollection of some sort of a mild, cold-like illness suffered by Liliane and her shortly following their encounter with the creature. Also, there was conflict in the testimony from Valquiria indicating the possibility that all three suffered an illness following the event. This will become more significant when I relate some of the other events pertinent to the Varginha case.

With reference to actual physical evidence, I drew a total blank. There was no obvious indication that any of the family could present me with anything even close to physical evidence.

Chapter 5

THE VARGINHA CASE UNFOLDS

EVENT # 2

Listening to Ubirajara originally explain what I refer to as the "first event" of the Varginha case, held us spellbound. I had interrupted the flow of his information to ask questions about the three girls and other aspects of the case. Although his answers were informative, they raised more questions. He emphasized many times that the entire case was filled with rumors and contradicting testimony from some of the witnesses.

Beca came into the room and said that Bira had a telephone call. He excused himself and told us he would be right back. In the interim, Beca brought an ample supply of refreshments for us to enjoy.

Soon Bira was back and continued the interview. He started by explaining that there is no particular order in which he relates the case and would gladly talk about the specific events I was interested in. Bira knew I had been terribly interested in the Varginha story for some time and had read all the available literature as well as having had conversations with John Mack and some of the other Brazilian investigators. I thanked him for his offer and decided to question him regarding the events as I had them ordered in my mind. The interview went as follows:

"Bira, could you please tell us next about the capture of the ET by the two military police officers?"

He answered, "I would be happy to go over that event. On the same day of January the 20th, around six o'clock in the evening, there was a rather violent hailstorm, which was unusual for that time of the year. It hit Varginha with a vengeance, breaking windows, windshields of cars, and causing all sorts of damage around town. It also resulted in destroying the footprints and other traces of the creature that was seen by the three girls on that afternoon. It was during this storm when two military police officers, traveling in their military police vehicle, spotted another creature. This entity resembled the one described by the three young women seen earlier the same day. It is possible this is the same creature, but no one actually knows for sure. According to eyewitness testimony, the being was seen trying to cross a street corner. It was limping and in some apparent physical distress. The two policemen pulled their vehicle over to the side, stopped, and one of them got out and ran over to the creature. I was told it seemed to give no resistance as the officer gently assisted it into the back seat of the automobile. The police officer, who was in his twenties, stopped by his mother's house. He was soaked to the skin from the rain. He told her he would have to work all night and asked her to notify his wife and tell her that he would not be home for dinner. At that point he changed his clothes and left. The spot where this event happened had been relatively close to where the three girls had seen the creature earlier in the day—about one and half blocks from where the first creature was seen. It's a good bet that the second creature that was captured by the two military police officers was indeed the same one seen by the girls."

In my opinion this makes a great deal of sense, as the description of the creature indicated it may have been injured. Perhaps this is why it was in a kneeling position when seen by the girls. Also, Liliane had a feeling that the creature might have been suffering. Another important factor is that it gave no resistance to its capture. Perhaps this also is related to the injury.

Bira continued, "It is believed this was the creature that was then taken to a small medical facility. By U.S. standards, the facility was the same as a small first-aid station without a support staff of physicians. The creature was examined in this facility and the men were told they could do little for it. They were advised to transport the creature to a full-fledged hospital. The police officers then drove to a small hospital in the heart of the city called Hospital Regional. Once the creature had been taken to this facility, little is known of what actually happened to it." (This part of the story I will cover later in this text and relates to a personal interview we did with some of the hospital staff.)

Bira went on to cover facts from the testimony of both the military and civilian witnesses: "The exact length of the creature's stay at Hospital Regional is unknown, but we do know that on Monday, January the 22nd, the creature was removed from the hospital by military personnel and imme-diately taken to another large hospital, called Hospital Humanitas, about one and a half miles away from the Hospital Regional. It is the most well equipped facility in the region. About 18 hours later a convoy of military vehicles was seen gathering at the back door of the Hospital Humanitas. Eyewitness talk about seeing a small box or coffin-like container being loaded on to a flatbed truck and then seeing a body placed in that container. Once this was done the convoy took off for an army-training base called Escola de Sargento Das Armas (ESA) in the town of Tres Coracoes, which is about 25 kilometers from Varginha. It was also noted that two soldiers [6 total] operated each of the three trucks. The operation for removal of the corpse was under the control of Army Military Intelligence called "S-2". This group is famous for being violent and oppressive. On Tuesday, January 23rd, the convoy left Tres Coracoes at 4 PM in the afternoon for Campinas in Sao Paulo state, where the cargo would be delivered to another military unit, possibly Escola Preparatoria De Cadetes. This part of the operation was commanded by Lieutenant Colonel Olimpio Wanderey Santos. Once the convoy reached its destination in Campinas, the corpse was delivered to the University of Campinas, one of the finest educational institutions in Brazil. After arrival and according to reliable eyewitness testimony, the ET body was autopsied by Dr. Badan Palhares, who has world-wide acclaim and gained notoriety for the autopsy performed some years ago which identified the bones of a famous German Nazi Criminal, Joseph Mengele. In a later interview with Dr. Palhares he denied having anything to do with any such ET operation. He also made a comment to one of his students in which he stated it would be a good number of years before he would be free to talk about his involvement with ETs. At the time when all this was occurring in Campinas, there were witnesses who described a United States military presence. It has been rumored that all physical evidence involved in the Varginha case has been transported to secret facilities in the United States."

As I previously stated, numerous Brazilian UFO investigators have become involved in the Varginha case. Certainly one of the most qualified is Mr. A. J. Gevaerd, the editor and director of Brazilian *UFO Magazine* and the Brazilian Center for Flying Saucer Research. The following is a quote from Mr. Gevaerd: "In reference to the incident in Varginha, I have learned that a few nurses and other personnel from Regional General Hospital had confirmed some facts and they were all suppressed. Individuals who had contacts with the second creature were advised to avoid the press and UFO researchers and are not to talk about it with anyone, not ever, including their families or relations. At the Humanitas Hospital, the second creature was kept at least two days and on the second night, on January 22nd, a huge military operation took place to remove the creature, already dead."

Interviews with some of the military who participated in the transportation of the creature from Hospital Humanitas declared that three trucks were used, each one driven by two different soldiers. It is believed that three trucks were used to remove only one body in order to avoid the involved personnel from knowing which truck actually was carrying the corpse. The drivers and their fellow personnel couldn't see the details of the operation, as they were kept outside the hospital area. Military personnel from the Army Internal Intelligence Corps were responsible for getting the corpse from the interior of the hospital, placing it into a box, and then on to one of the trucks. All three trucks were then taken to a military facility in Campinas, state of Sao Paulo, about 200 miles from Varginha, in the middle of the night. There, the corpse was moved to the University of Campinas, one of the best institutions in the country. It is believed, and now confirmed through detailed information, that the ET body was autopsied by Dr. Baden Palhares.

UFO researchers from all over the country have been helping Rodrigues and Pacaccini in order to discover each and every detail of the capture of the two ETs. Media in Brazil have never been so active, and great majorities of the population believe that the case is real and the military and civil authorities involved are keeping the facts secret. Many strange events were happening simultaneously, such as the imprisonment of some military personnel, sergeants being transferred at short notice, etc. The phones of many UFO researchers involved in the case are confirmed to be tapped and have received anonymous threats.

Up to now the UFO researchers know almost all the details of the whole operation and a few can be released to the public. The researchers in many cities are receiving new pieces of this fantastic puzzle every day, and more and more military personnel are agreeing to talk. Meanwhile, the region where Varginha is geographically located (in the south of the state of Minas Gerais) is subject to one of the biggest UFO waves ever registered, complete with huge UFOs in close observation, landings and contacts.

A Trip to the Wall

It was about one o'clock in the afternoon. We had taken the morning and early afternoon for the initial interview with Ubirajara. I was excited to have received all the important information from the person whom I considered the leading authority on the case. Bira suggested we take a break for lunch and afterward he would take us to the areas where both the first and second events had taken place. Phil was excited about this. It was his first exposure to this entire case and although he knew little about it, he kept an open mind.

We dismantled and repacked the camera equipment in preparation for the afternoon's activity. It was loaded into the car and we were soon on our way to a local restaurant. During lunch the conversation involved more of the events that had taken place. I made mental notes so I could ask questions when the interview continued.

It was only a short drive through a residential neighborhood until we parked the car. Bira told us to take the cameras and make sure we had the tripod. We followed his advice and followed him up a small hill through an area of houses, which appeared to be in the moderate-income bracket. The housing was dense without visible vacant areas of land or empty lots. Once at the top of the hill, we crossed a small narrow street. Directly ahead of us was a wall, about eight feet in height, composed of gray concrete blocks. Smack-dab in the middle of this wall was a rather strange appearing metallic door.

The metal wall showing the locked door. This was built to con-ceal the area where the alien being was kneeling.

The door was secured with a chain and a large keyed padlock. Bira explained that behind this door and the wall was a vacant lot. This was the very spot where the three girls saw the creature. I asked him why they built this wall and who built it. He answered that somebody did not want investi-gators or outsiders coming into the area and decided to block it from view. He did not know who was responsible for building the wall and had no idea who held the key to the metallic door. He suggested we mount the camera on the tripod and volunteered to lift this combination into the air and manipulate it so we could video the area where the creature was kneeling. Since there was no direct access, I thought this was a good suggestion and did as he advised. He lifted the tripod with the camera running into the air and point-ed the lens over the wall, turning the camera in various directions and angles so that we had the possibility of actually capturing the spot where the crea-ture was kneeling. Suddenly an elderly man exited his house next door and approached us. He was probably in his late seventies, had a short beard, and gave the appearance of a rough and gruff individual. He exchanged words with Bira in Portuguese. All the time I was afraid we were in trouble for try-ing to take video of the other side of the wall. Rudolfo was smiling from ear to ear. I asked him what was going on. He told us this gentleman lived next door and he thought he might have a key that would fit the locked door. Both

Phil and I were very excited at this prospect. The neighbor briefly returned to the confines of his home and soon was back on the spot holding a large key ring, which must have at least contained fifty keys of various sizes and shapes. He immediately began trying them on the locked door. While this was going on we removed the camera from the tripod and began filming the houses and the street. Bira was explaining what direction the three young girls were coming from and where they were headed. We did our best to follow his explanation with the camera. This was very important and would add to the documentation of the case.

Translator Rodolpho and Dr. Leir at the spot where the three
girls saw alien being.

From out of the blue, we heard a shout and turned to see the neighbor pushing on the metal door. It swung open with a bang, hitting the wall on the other side. He had successfully managed to find a key that fit the lock. Bira led the way. He was first through the opening and we followed on his heels. On the other side of the wall was just an open, vacant field with a ground cover of mixed grass and weeds. The distant end of the field was open onto the surrounding hillside where no houses or other structures had yet been built. To our left was another concrete wall that appeared much older and showed the wear of time. It was stained with various colors and showed rain damage, as well as damage from numerous other sources. This was the exact spot where the creature was kneeling. Bira went over to a spot by this wall and knelt on the ground, imitating the position of the being the girls had seen. He showed us the exact spot where he had seen impressions in the soft soil and where he found the mysterious small, round hole. Phil was busy recording all

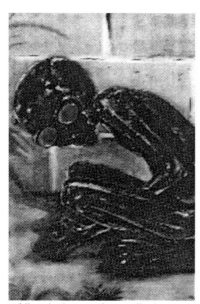

Alien being at the wall, drawn by eyewitness.

this with the video camera. I grabbed the still camera and asked Bira if he would again assume the position he had previously demonstrated. He kindly did so and I proceeded to take numerous still photos of the area for documentation. Bira told us about the rapid growth in Varginha and its ever-expanding population. He explained the area we were in was one of those dense centers of growth. For some unknown reason this vacant lot was set aside and nothing was allowed to be built on it. He did not know who was responsible for this decision, either. Once we had finished filming, Bira thanked the older gentleman for opening the door for us. We left the confines of this secluded area and went back onto the sidewalk outside.

Bira then told us to set the camera up on the sidewalk and film him as he walked down the street. Without understanding what he was up to, we did as he asked. With the camera rolling we watched as he walked about two blocks down the street to an intersection. Once he reached this spot he turned toward the camera and began waiving his arms in the air. I couldn't understand what he wanted but we kept the camera rolling, with him in the viewfinder. He then stopped waiving his arms and began his trek back to us. Since it was uphill all the way, he returned short of breath and explained to Rudolfo that the spot he was at was where the two military police officers had picked up the second creature. Once we understood how close this actually was to where the young girls first saw the creature, we were totally convinced this was the same creature they had seen a few hours earlier in the day. Bira went on to explain that this is one of the reasons why the number of creatures had been rumored to be more than what were actually involved in the case.

It was now about 3:30 in the afternoon. We were filled with knowledge and excitement. I had to make a decision to stop for the day or continue with more interviews. I asked Bira if he felt up to a short continuation of his interview. He agreed and we returned to his Institute.

Back at the Institute we re-established our camera positions and continued with Bira's interview.

"Ubirajara, is there more to the story about the two military police officers who picked up the second creature?"

Bira continued, which added more mystery to the case. "Within two weeks after these officers picked up the creature, one of them died of an unknown condition. This deceased military police officer left behind a wife and two children. He died in the hospital and numerous rumors abound pertaining to his cause of death. Supposedly, there was no death certificate issued, no medical records available, and no witnesses willing to talk about the situation. A television production company from the U.K. came to Varginha the year following the incident and performed an investigation of the case. The resultant program was only shown in the U.K. One of the individuals they interviewed was the sister of the deceased military police officer. On camera she had stated her brother had a high fever, was dehydrated, could not eat, had bleeding from certain areas of his body, and finally was unable to remain conscious or communicate.

I was shocked to hear about these symptoms, as they sounded suspiciously similar to symptoms associated with an Ebola virus infection. Could it be possible that these creatures harbor microorganisms that might be fatal to humans? If this were true, then the possibility of open contact between ETs and humans suddenly becomes more complicated. Everyone always envisions the meeting of ETs and humans by the popular concept of the landing of an alien craft on the White House lawn in Washington, D.C. Suppose such a meeting did take place and the visitors harbored numerous microorganisms that could be fatal to the human race. Such a meeting could result in the total annihilation of mankind. Is it possible that our visitors know this and take measures to prevent such a calamity from taking place? Numerous alien abductees talk about being placed in some kind of cylindrical container with some sort of fluid in it that they were forced to breathe. It is a terrifying experience. Is it possible this fluid treatment prevents microorganisms from crossing over from one species to another and therefore prevents contamination of either species? I believe the information coming from this Brazilian case may provide some explanation for, and enlightenment on, the subject of interactions with non-terrestrial species.

I asked Bira if he personally did any investigation at the hospital in reference to the death of this military police officer. He stated he did go there and was not able to obtain any information whatsoever. According to Bira, all medical records were confiscated by the military and that no one in the hospital would speak about the case. After hearing this, it became clear that the information in reference to this mysterious death would not be forthcoming and I decided to not pursue it further. I thanked Bira for the interview he gave us and hoped we could continue it tomorrow or the next day.

As we began to dismantle the recording equipment the telephone rang and Bira was called from the room. He received at least a dozen phone calls within the next half hour. Rudolfo came back into the room and explained that his father had just received some amazing telephone calls. It seemed the word had gotten out regarding me—that there was a doctor from the United States visiting the area who was looking into the ET case. He told us his father would be back in a few minutes and tell us what was going on.

Bira returned to the room and was very excited, as the gleam in his eyes was a sure giveaway of his personal feelings. Through Rodolfo's translation, he told us a major Brazilian television network had just called and requested an interview with me. The audience for this network reached far and wide in South America. It would involve millions of people watching and listening to what I had to say. He asked if I was willing to do the show and I replied that I had done several thousand hours of TV in the past and would be more than happy to accommodate them. I also explained that I was his guest and my time was his, so he could arrange for this to happen at any time he wished. He thanked me and went to the next subject. It seemed that not only television wanted me for an interview but also several local radio stations. I also agreed to do the radio shows and told him I would go along with any arrangements he made. Bira was still excited and explained again, through Rudolfo, that there were some new witnesses that just came forward and agreed to be interviewed by me. One of these witnesses, coincidentally enough, just happened to be the wife of the deceased military police officer. I stood there in a mild state of shock, as this certainly was a strange synchronistic event. I advised Bira to set up her interview as soon as possible, suggesting the possibility of it occurring the very the next day. He told me he would get in touch with her and arrange it. I was divinely elated by this new turn of events. Little did I know that Bira was not finished with his news yet.

"By the way", he stated through Rudolfo, "I have more news. I also just received a call from some medical personnel who were working at Hospital Regional during the time when the military brought in the non-terrestrial being. They also would like to talk with you. They do not want to be filmed or recorded, nor do they want their names used or to be quoted anywhere in Brazil, as they are terrified for possible retribution from the authorities. They are also afraid for their lives. They have not talked about this to anyone for six years and have kept this information strictly to themselves. It has been a terrible burden for them. They have agreed to talk to me, Rudolfo, you and Phil. No one else may be present. Please tell me, are you willing to talk with them?"

I was overcome with emotion and elation. "I would be more than happy to talk with them and would agree to whatever conditions they ask for. Please relay my assurances that they would have complete anonymity."

He excused himself and went back to the telephone. I assumed he was providing the answers to those who had previously called. About one hour later we were on our way to dinner and back to the hotel for the night.

The following morning Phil and I returned to Bira's Institute and were notified that he had made arrangements to interview the wife of the deceased military police officer. This officer, Marco Eli Cherese, was only 23 years of age when he succumbed to what is believed to be an illness caused by his direct contact with an alien being. We were told she would arrive at 10:30 AM. We convened a planning session and decided on what questions to ask. I inquired if she spoke or understood English and was told that she did not. Therefore, we agreed to use the original set-up we had used for Bira's interview. I would sit in the middle seat with the witness on one side, and then Rudolfo would translate from the other seat. Phil would man the camera and record the entire interview. I was extremely enthusiastic as it would be an opportunity to learn many details pertaining to the mysterious death of the involved individual.

On the stroke of 10:30, the doorbell sounded. Beca responded, and I heard conversation in the hall. We were introduced to Mrs. Cherese. She was small in stature and slight of build. She had medium length, straight black hair and a pale, olive-skinned complexion. I shook her delicate hand and welcomed her to the interview. Through Rudolfo, I thanked her for being there and for her anticipated answers to my questions. At no time during our initial meeting did she show any change in facial expression, and she remained rather stone-faced through the entire interview.

Dr. L: Mrs. Cherese, I want you to just sit back and relax. I thank you so very much again for being here with us today and commend you for agreeing to let me ask you a few questions. Let me begin by asking you how long your husband was in the hospital before he passed away?

Mrs. C: I believe he was in there less than one week.

Dr. L: How long was he sick at home before he went to the hospital?

Mrs. C: I don't remember.

Dr. L: Can you tell us what his symptoms were when he was ill at home?

Mrs. C: I don't know.

Dr. L: Do you remember the night he came home during the rainstorm?

Mrs. C: Yes.

Dr. L: What happened that night?

Mrs. C: He had stopped at his mother's first and didn't come home till much later than usual. He was just out doing his job. Then he left to go back to work.

Dr. L: Did he tell you what he was doing on that night?

Mrs. C: No, he never told about his work. It was military work.

Dr. L: How was he feeling that night?

Mrs. C: He was overworked, tired, cold, and had to go back out and go back to work.

Dr. L: How long did it take after that when he became ill?

Mrs. C: I don't remember.

Dr. L: Do you recall how long he was ill before he went to the hospital?

Mrs. C: I really don't remember.

Dr. L: Did you visit your husband when he was in the hospital?

Mrs. C: Yes.

Dr. L: What were his symptoms when you saw him in the hospital?

Mrs. C: I don't know.

Dr. L: Did you at any time see his medical records or talk with the doctors that were taking care of him.

Mrs. C: No.

Dr. L: After his death, did you ask for a copy of the medical records?

Mrs. C: Yes, but they didn't give them to me.

Dr. L: Did they give you a copy of his death certificate?

Mrs. C: No.

Dr. L: Did you ask for one?

Mrs. C: Yes I did, but I never got one.

Dr. L: Did you go to his funeral?

Mrs. C: No.

Dr. L: Why was this? Surely you wanted to be there.

Mrs. C: Of course I did, but I was not told anything about the funeral. It was all secret and handled by the military.

Dr. L: Did any members of either your family or his family visit him in the hospital?

Mrs. C: I don't know.

Dr. L: Did any of them receive a copy of his medical records or a copy of the death certificate?

Mrs. C: No.

Dr. L: Were you told or was anyone told why your husband died? Was what his cause of death?

Mrs. C: None of us were told anything.

Dr. L: Please forgive me for asking you, but do you receive any compensation from the Brazilian military or any branch of the Brazilian government?
Mrs. C: No.

Dr. L: If that is the case, then how are you able to take care of your children and pay your expenses?

Mrs. C: I don't know. It is difficult.

Dr. L: I think that concludes the questions I have for you. I want to thank
you so very much for coming and letting me interview you. I am sure you are very brave and hope you are able to get along well in the future.

With the final answer to my question, we concluded the interview. Both Bira and I thanked her once again for coming and talking with us.

Discussion

After considering all aspects of the interview and what I had previously learned about the case, I was led to the conclusion that there were more complications and confusion involved than just rumors. I found the testimony of the deceased military police officer's wife to be most illuminating, not because she came forth with readily usable information, but actually the direct opposite. Watching her movements during the questioning was most interesting because it was obvious, even to a non-student of NLP, that she was hiding a great deal of information. Her negative comments indicated a high probability of intimidation and resultant fear, perhaps generated by the military or other representatives of the Brazilian government. She appeared a very gentle soul with a deep internal conflict about telling us the full story, or even a smattering of the truth. When her testimony is contrasted with that of the deceased's sister, one can easily see that the events proceeding and following her brother's death were destined to remain a secret.

This second event, in its entirety, illustrates the complexity of the case from the very beginning. From the time when the two police officers picked up the creature, made a stop at one of their homes, and finally escorted the entity to it's second destination at Hospital Regional, the case continued to grow in complexity.

Chapter 6

THE MEDICAL TESTIMONY

I was catapulted from a sound, deep sleep into an awakened state by the ringing of the telephone at 8:00 AM. I answered the call in my usual morning gruff voice. On the line was Rudolfo, who seemed excited and asked if we were up and about yet. He asked how long it would be before he and his father could pick us up and I told him about an hour. I asked him what he was so excited about. He explained that his father had made arrangements with some medical personnel who had worked at Hospital Regional at the time when the humanoid being was there, to be interviewed by me. He told me they had scheduled this for approximately 11:00 AM and wanted to know if the timing met with our approval. I told him I saw no problem with the time and thanked him for arranging the interview. With that, I was told they would pick us up at the hotel in an hour. I tossed the receiver back on the cradle and shouted at Phil to wake up. He was usually the first one out of bed and seemed shocked I was already up and advancing to the shower. I explained the essence of the phone call and that we had to be ready in one hour.

Bira and Rudolfo arrived on time and we headed out for parts unknown. I asked where the interview was going to take place and was told it would be in a medical office close to the hospital.

We were soon in the downtown area of the city. As with all cities anywhere in the world, the sites were essentially the same: multiple shops and a mix of tall buildings and individual stores. The sidewalks appeared heavily traveled with pedestrians and surprisingly, there were no obvious signs of a depressed economy. Brazil, even with its financial woes, showed no internal signs of depression. I found it strange that in the face a constant devaluing dollar and increasing inflationary pressure, the economy outwardly appeared stable and strong.

Bira slowed the car to a crawl and Rudolfo told us we were now passing Hospital Regional. I asked if we could return later and video the facility, and he said it would be no problem. We proceeded for a few more blocks and turned into what appeared to be a very wide alley. Again Bira slowed to a stop and Rudolfo explained that we were at the rear entrance of Humanitas Hospital. This was where the military vehicles were seen with what appeared to be a coffin containing the deceased EBE. I asked if we could return to this area also at a later time for filming purposes and he wholeheartedly agreed. We proceeded down the alley and came out onto a small business street. I noticed a sign in Portuguese which was indicating a medical facility; I assumed this could have been the rendezvous point. Bira pulled the car to the curb and parked. Rudolfo was the first to exit the vehicle and asked us follow along as they proceeded into the building. We entered what appeared to be a medical waiting room, in which there were several straight back chairs along the walls of the room and a table in the center with piles of magazines in Portuguese. One of the walls had an open sliding glass window with a number of forms placed on a clipboard sitting on the counter. I assumed we had arrived in this medical facility during their lunch hour, as no personnel were present. Bira called out in Portuguese and in a few moments the door swung open. Standing there was a gentleman wearing a white doctor's coat. There was a friendly exchange between the two men. Bira turned toward Phil and myself and the introductions were made. It was evident that the doctor did not speak English. He gestured for us to follow him down a hallway and soon we were in what appeared to be a conference room. The room was more long than wide and had an elongated, shiny wooden conference table surrounded by matching chairs. The walls were adorned with a number certificates indicating various medical diplomas. Although they were all in Portuguese, I was able to read the names and determine what specialty was indicated. At this point an intense conversation began between Bira and the doctor. An innate feeling of uneasiness suddenly overwhelmed me. The tension began to increase. Rudolfo explained to us that the doctor was still concerned about revealing information to anyone for fear of reprisal. About five minutes passed and two other individuals entered the room. One gentleman was in his late fifties, heavyset, with curly gray hair, and one dark-haired lady, also wearing a long white doctor's coat. Introductions were made and we all took seats. At that point another lengthy conversation took place between the witnesses and Bira. We sat quietly and listened without understanding a word of their discussion. Rudolfo finally explained what this was all about. As suspected, it seemed they were still fearful about releasing the information and were concerned it could prove dangerous to them—not only because they were warned never to discuss the subject, but also because of threats against their license. The next fact presented to us by Rudolfo shocked me to the core. They told Bira there were threats that had been made against them and their families. At this point I could fully understand their trepidation. They wanted us to agree that this information would not be publicized in Brazil and that their names would never be used. They told Bira they were still being watched and if there was any indication that they had made statements to us, things could go very badly for them. We gave our assurances that we would fulfill their requests. The atmosphere in the room at that point was so thick you could cut through it with a knife. I could feel the tension internally.

The first statements came from the doctor we initially had met. He said that all they were about to divulge had nothing to do with them personally, but were rumors they had heard from friends working in the hospital at the time. He denied having any personal knowledge whatsoever. Rudolfo explained to them that we understood and would accept whatever they had to tell us in that light.

The Interview

In order to simplify the narration, I will present this testimony with one collective voice instead of all the parties involved. The answers to my questions will be the interpretation by Rudolfo. The doctor and his colleagues will be referred to as "MP" (Medical Personnel) and, as with previous interviews, I will be designated as Dr. L.

Dr. L: Could you please verify that the events in question had occurred on the night of January 20th, 1996?

MP: Yes, that is the correct date.

Dr. L: Could you please start by telling us what initially happened that night that made you think there was something unusual happening?

MP: First of all, we would like to explain we do not have first-hand knowledge of what happened. We were told about certain things that happened in the hospital, but we don't have any first-hand knowledge.

At that point, it was obvious this was going to be an emotionally charged interview. The expressions on their faces appeared strained. I got the distinct feeling that there was going to be more to this than would meet the eye. It should also be understood that my emotions were also on edge. I couldn't imagine what they were going to tell us, but I knew I was on to something of grave importance.

Dr. L: Please go ahead and tell us what happened or what you heard happened.

MP: Well, all was going pretty much routine for us when we noticed a few military people around in the halls. We did not feel this was unusual because sometimes there were accidents involving the military and some of the guys came in for treatment or just to be with the guy who was injured. You know, car accidents and things like that—nothing that was too serious, usually. We continued going about our business. The hospital was not really very busy that night as we had only about half the beds occupied and weren't seeing any emergencies coming in. We were told by one of the surgical orderlies that there were some military vehicles pulling up in the back of the hospital. We really didn't find that unusual either. Please understand most of this has to do with what we heard, rumors and talk.

Dr. L: Did you her about any unusual activity going on in the surgery area of the hospital?

MP: There was an increase in the number of military people and it looked like people were not free to go where they wanted in the hospital.

Dr. L: What do you mean by that?

MP: Well, there were people we knew who worked in the surgery area and they weren't allowed to go in there.

Dr. L: Can you tell us what exactly was stopping them from entering the area?

MP: There were military guards posted at the doors and they weren't letting anybody in or out. Once you were in there you couldn't get out, not even if you had to go to the bathroom.

Dr. L: What was happening inside the surgical area?

MP: People were running around. Everybody was in a state of panic. There was no order to anything. Mass confusion. The military was very dominating. We knew they brought a patient in through the back door of the hospital and brought them directly into surgery. We thought there must have been a really bad accident on the base. The other thing that really upset us was that we were told not to talk about this to anyone once it was all over. We were strongly warned from the beginning.

Dr. L: Can you tell us what specifically was going on in that area of the hospital?

MP: Yes, we were preparing for a surgery but no one knew what kind of a surgery or who the patient was. They had taken the patient directly into one of the operating rooms.

Dr. L: Can you tell us what your specialty is?

MP: Yes, it's orthopedic surgery.

The mood of the witnesses suddenly changed; they appeared more nervous and began looking at each other. I also noted a change in attitude from individuals who were supposed to be the recipients of rumors and third-party comments to actual first-hand witnesses and participants. I looked about the room and could see Bira, Rudolfo and Phil sitting on the edge of their seats, waiting for the next bombshell. I kept these observations to myself and went on with the interview.

Dr. L: Please go ahead and tell us what happened next.

MP: I was asked to begin a surgical scrub and to prepare for a fracture reduction. I inquired as to what part of the body had sustained the fracture and was simply told it was the leg. The answers came from one of the military officers. I noticed two armed officers were guarding the entrance to one of the operating suites and assumed the patient was already on the table being prepped for the surgery. Some of the nursing personnel were going about their business with little resistance from the military. It was also a bit disconcerting to see military personnel armed with weapons and live ammunition inside the operating areas of our hospital. We did not have this experience with any of the previous military accident cases.

Dr. L: Were you presented with any kind of a medical record of the patient or did anyone tell you the full extent of his injuries or even the vital signs?

MP: No, there was no information available. Another strange thing was there was no conversation occurring between any of the hospital staff or the military. Everybody was acting really strange. There were times when other military personnel would come into the area and have short exchanges of conversation in a very low tone so you could not hear what they were talking about; just loud enough to be not quite a whisper.

Dr. L: What happened next after you finished your scrub?

MP: We were handed sterile towels and dried our hands. Next the military guard opened the operating room doors and we were told to enter. The patient was already on the table and covered to the neck with a sterile drape sheet. Two of the operating room nurses were preparing to gown us. Our back was still turned away from the patient. I noticed that the expression on the faces of the nursing personnel was very peculiar. I would guess you could say they had a look of terror in their eyes.

Dr. L: Did you have any conversation with the nurses?

MP: We only asked them to hand us what we needed, such as surgical gloves. I also asked if some of the needed equipment was in the room that I usually used for my fracture reductions.

Dr. L: Please continue.

MP: I turned around and approached the operating table with my colleagues. At first glance I noticed the patient was quite small and my first impression was that it was a child. I thought perhaps a military dependent had an accident and was brought into the facility for surgical treatment. We slowly approached the table. When I first saw the face of the individual lying there I was in a state of shock. It was far from a human face; certainly no face I had ever seen before. The eyes were large and red and staring at the ceiling with a blank stare. I turned and looked at my colleagues. We were all dumbfounded. One of the military officers of a high rank was in the room. He told us the victim on the table had suffered a fractured leg and we were to " fix it". His tone was commanding and far from a request. I asked him for some details regarding the patient and was told I was not there to ask questions but to only perform the requested task. He also told us to do the best job we could and to disregard the circumstances at hand. We were also advised to solve any problem that might arise, no matter what the nature. His closing remarks were even more severe and emotionally upsetting. We were told not to come out of the room until the operation was over. Any questions or requests would be relayed through the military personnel on the other side of the operating room doors. We turned and looked at each other and could not believe this was happening. With that, he turned and left the room.

Dr. L: At that point in time did you think this individual lying on the operating table was some sort of circus freak, malformed child, or perhaps something in the animal kingdom?

MP: We really didn't know what to think. One of the things we decided to do was to get a better look at the surgery sight and at the same time examine the patient. It was at this point, when we threw back the drape cover, that we realized this creature was probably not of this world. Earlier in the day we had heard rumors of some kids seeing an unusual creature in town as well as hearing about other military activity around town.

Drawing of alien creature by eyewitness.

Dr. L: Can you describe to us what this creature looked like?

MP: Yes. The being was less than five feet tall. It was bipedal with two arms and two legs. The color of the skin was a dark brown, which appeared rather shiny; like it was oily or wet but in fact the skin was dry. The skin also looked reticulated, like large scales but when you touched it, the demarcations of scales were not present. It was smooth to the touch. One of the most noticeable features was that of the head. It was large, much too large for the size of the individual. There were three bony protuberances on the top of the head, one in each parietal area and one central. They extended from the frontal to the occipital portions, like ridges. There was no hair present either on the head or the rest of the body. The head was also larger in its upper portion than lower toward the jaw area. The eyes were large, slightly upturned toward the lateral aspects, oriental looking. They were red in color and looked like two glimmering pools of liquid. For some reason all of us did not want to look into this creature's eyes and refrained from doing so. There was a very small remnant of a mouth and two little openings with a slight ridge where his nose should have been. There were no noted ears, only small openings that looked like vestigial ear canals. The neck was narrow in diameter and appeared it would not have enough muscular strength to support such a large head. The upper portion of the torso was slight of build with an obvious rib cage. There were no noted breasts, areola or nipples. The abdomen was similar to that of a human with the absence of a naval. The upper thigh portions were muscular and out of proportion to the rest of the torso. This was totally different from the arms, which were thin and emaciated. The hands ended in four fingers with no thumb. The fingers were strange and different than human fingers. The creature was able to move each of his fingers so that they could articulate with each other, and by doing so, was able to probably perform all the functions we could with the use of our thumbs. We were not able to tell whether these fingers were multi-jointed or for some reason the bones were flexible, enabling the fingers to perform their desired functions. The upper leg and thighs ended in what appeared to be similar to a human knee joint with an oversized patella. The lower portions of the leg were also similar to that of a human. The entire lower extremities were heavily endowed with muscles. It crossed my mind that wherever this creature had come from, the gravity might have been much more than here on earth. The foot was narrow and fleshy. There were three short fleshy toes that looked more like pads than toes. There were no visible toenails or fingernails. There was an additional appendage that hung down from the medial side of the foot. This vestigial appendage was elongated like a finger and ended in what appeared to be a claw about three quarters of an inch long. Later we found when the being walked, it would move this appendage so it became parallel to the rest of the foot. This allowed it to ambulate in a normal human-like manner.

Dr. L: Did you examine the sight of the injury?

MP: Yes, it was in the upper thigh and involved a compound fracture of the femur. The bone was protruding from the skin and there had been some bleeding around the sight of the wound, which had clotted and was dry.

Dr. L: Were there x-rays taken and did you view the x-rays?

MP: Yes, they were up on the view screen in the surgery room. It showed a clear view of the fractured bone.

Dr. L: Was the fracture visible on the x-rays and did you feel it could be reduced in the manner you would use to treat human fractures?

MP: Yes, it was clearly visible and I believed it could be treated in the same manner as we treat human fractures.

Dr. L: Was the patient awake or conscious and was there any attempt at

communication?

MP: The patient was apparently awake. It kept moving its head but mainly stared upward at the ceiling. We did make an attempt to communicate verbally but did not receive an answer. We were concerned as to whether it was feeling any pain, but we really had no way of knowing. When we examined the fracture sight it did not jerk away, scream, or give any sign of discomfort.

Dr. L: Was the patient given any kind of an anesthetic for the procedure?

MP: We had decided not to use a general anesthesia because we didn't know anything about its metabolism. We thought perhaps any of our gases might kill the thing. We were even afraid to administer oxygen because no one knew what kind of an atmosphere it was used to. We decided to try a small amount of local anesthesia and see if there was any untoward effect. Fortunately there was not and that is how we were able to do the procedure.

Dr. L: Could you please tell us about the procedure, the blood, the bone, etc.? What color was the blood? Was it blue or green?

MP: To our surprise the blood was dark red, just like our blood. When the blood was examined under the microscope we found the cellular structure to be very similar to human blood with the exception of the platelet count being much higher in number. We also found the blood would coagulate immediately upon release from a blood vessel. We were not able to determine whether this was due to the high platelet count or whether the creature was in a different atmosphere than it was used to.

Dr. L: Was the bone also similar to ours?

MP: Yes, with the exception that it was pinker in color and contained numerous lacunae or holes, giving it the appearance of osteoporotic human bone. Another difference was its tensile strength. It was much stronger than human bone. We did not find it necessary to use stabilization devices to fixate the fracture site. Once the bone ends were approximated, the fracture defect seemed to stabilize and could not be moved apart.

Dr. L: Did the patient at anytime make any noise, cry out in pain, or object to the treatment?

MP: No, it remained very still. Its respirations were shallow, as if it needed very little air to sustain life.

Dr. L: Could you detect a heartbeat or pulse?

MP: That is a good question. We tried to determine exactly that and we could not tell. Sometimes we thought we could hear a heart beat and then at other times it was absent; we found the same with the detection of a pulse.

At this point we decided to take a short break in the questioning. The room was steeped in silence. We all looked at each other with wonderment in our eyes. The medical personnel sat silently, immersed in deep thoughts. Their faces seemed strained and ashen in color. It was as if their faces had been drained of blood. A brief period of conversation erupted between Rudolfo and Bira. I could not understand, as they were conversing in their native language. I looked at Phil. He looked at me in disbelief. I made some comment to him about the time and we had a brief bout of idle conversation pertaining to dinner plans.

About ten minutes passed. We all seemed more relaxed and I took a large swig of water and asked: "Well, why don't we get back to the subject at hand, so these folks can get on with their daily tasks?"

Bira made a statement in Portuguese and Rudolfo asked me to carry on with the next question.

Dr. L: Is there anything else you can add to what you have already told us about the creature?

There was a brief moment of silence before the orthopedist began his answer.

MP: There was an incident that happened but I hesitate to tell you about it because it is so strange you might not believe me. Honestly, as a doctor you will realize I am telling you nothing but the truth.

Dr. L: Please go ahead. I trust what you are saying is the truth.

MP: When we had finished the surgery for repair of the fracture, we were still highly tense. We did not know how the patient was going to respond to what we had done to it. We were also afraid if something untoward happened to the creature, we would get the blame from the military and the punishment might be severe. Those thoughts were going through my head. Suddenly, out of nowhere the room began to fill with a greenish mist. We all stepped back from the operating table. We did not immediately know the origin of this mist and feared it might be toxic. One of the operating room nurses began frantically banging on the operating room door. A voice on the other side inquired if we were finished with the surgery. We told them we were essentially finished but there seemed to be greenish gas collecting in the room and we did not know the origin. With that, there was some heated conversation outside of the operating room and we were told to find the origin of the greenish substance and let them know. We did not know at this point whether it was a gas, vapor or mist but finally realized it seemed to be emanating from the creature lying on the table. In deep fear, I walked slowly closer to it and approached the head of the table. Without consciously realizing it, my gaze caught the eyes of the being. His eyes were glowing red and appeared as two swirling pools of liquid. They were pulling, pulling me in, deeper and deeper. All at once giant portions of information came pounding into my head. These were like thought grams, large blocks of information. Over and over and over, like someone hitting me in the head with a hammer. I was also becoming dizzy and slightly nauseated.

Dr. L: Undoubtedly you survived this ordeal. Can you tell us what was in these thought messages?

MP: All that I am willing to tell you at this time is what the creature told me about human beings. I also want to tell you he downloaded a tremendous amount of knowledge into my head. It caused me to have headaches lasting for over two weeks following the event.

Dr. L: Please go ahead and tell us what he told you.

MP: Yes. Essentially he told me his race felt very sorry for the human beings for basically two reasons. The first is that all humans have the same potential and abilities to perform the very same things his race could do. Those things we find so marvelous and magical but humans did not know how to do them. For example he told me in cases where there is injury or disease of the body, it would not be necessary to confine one of his species to a special treatment facility such as the one he was confined in at the moment. He told me they either individually or joined together could produce all the healing necessary to repair their bodies. The second reason they felt sorry for us was we did not seem to realize we were spiritual beings only living in a temporary shell and we were totally disconnected from our spiritual self.

Dr. L: That is a fascinating piece of information. Can you tell us anything further that you learned?
MP: No, that is all we are willing to share at this time.

Dr. L: What happened to the creature when after you left the room?

MP: We checked on the being from time to time. It seemed stable and had a fantastic rate of healing. The wound healed completely in less than twenty-four hours. This was also true of the bone. It was completely mended within the same period of time.

Dr. L: What happened after the healing was complete?

MP: The military took the creature out the back door of the hospital.

Dr. L: What condition was the creature in when it left with its military escort?

MP: It was in *satisfactory medical condition.*

This is a standard term used in medical practice anywhere in the world to designate the status of a patient. It means the patient is alive with all vital signs are normal and well.

Dr. L: Are you using that terminology in the strict medical sense?

MP: Yes, the patient left the hospital in SATISFACTORY MED-
ICAL CONDITION.

Dr. L. Doctor, I want to thank you very much for the information
you and your colleagues have given us. I was wondering if there were
any x-rays or medical records available to look at?

MP: No there are no records available.

Dr. L. There certainly must have been records originally. If that was
the case, what happened to them?
MP: We believe the military confiscated all the records, x-rays, laboratory data and materials used.

Dr. L: Is there any chance that copies were made that they did not
get their hands on?
MP: I don't know.

With that, we concluded the interview. I looked intently at the physician
who had just completed the last portion of the testimony. He was sitting in a
chair, slightly bent over at the waist. Perspiration had formed on his brow
and was streaking downward through his sideburns. Tears were running
down his cheeks, his hands were extended in front of him, shaking, and he
was trembling and distraught. I approached him, gently placed my arm
around his shoulder and silently gave him a hug. Within a short period of
time they had recovered their composure. We thanked them again for taking
the time they had given us for the interview and reassured them that we
would not divulge what they had said or reveal their names anywhere in
Brazil.

Discussion
My intent in researching the Varginha case was to procure physical evidence or something of that nature which could be analyzed by the scientific
community. The more time I spent in Varginha, the more I became aware that
my chances of fulfilling my original goal were rapidly going from slim to
none. The medical testimony I had just attained was most gratifying and
shook me emotionally—but who would believe me without corroborating
their testimony? All considered, I believed this testimony could be the
strongest piece of evidence yet in the case. When I returned to the United
States I told their story to a number of individuals, some within the scientif-

ic establishment and some who were not. One of these people reacted in a way I shall always remember and that person was Robert Bigelow of the National Institute for Discovery Science. Shortly after my return from Brazil, I set up a meeting with Bob at his office in Las Vegas, Nevada. It was a casual meeting with a few of his scientific friends in attendance. He asked me what was new and I responded by telling him that I had recently returned from Brazil. He asked if I was there to attend or speak at conferences and I explained that I did speak at several conferences, but my main goal was to visit Varginha and make an attempt at acquiring physical evidence in that case. Since Bob constantly kept up to date on events in the UFO field, he knew immediately what case I was talking about. He inquired about my success in achieving my goal. I explained to him about returning without such evidence, but instead had performed interviews on eyewitnesses in the case, some who had already been interviewed and others who had not. He inquired about the particulars and I told him the story of the medical testimony. When I was finished telling the story, the room fell silent. One of his colleagues asked the following question with a smirking grin on his face: "Bob, do you believe what Dr. Leir has just told you?" Bob sat silently for a few seconds and then responded. "You know if anyone else other than Dr. Leir had told me this story, I would tend to have my doubts, but coming from him I believe every word." I found this to be a profound compliment and shall never forget it.

Chapter 7

THE VARGINHA CASE UNFOLDS

EVENT #3

Phil and I discussed the events of the day in our hotel room. I asked him if he believed the medical witnesses were telling the truth and he responded by saying their testimony impressed him because he was swayed by their emotional exhibition, which he felt was genuine. I also broached the subject pertaining to what they had told us in the very beginning of their interview, referencing statements about how they obtained their information by rumor, innuendo and passive conversation. Phil and I were of the same opinion—one that casts doubt on these statements. We both believed they were actual participants.

The following day we met Bira and Rudolfo for breakfast and then returned to the Institute to continue with Bira's interview, with Rudolfo doing the translation.

I asked Bira to explain what he personally considered to be the next most important event involving the case. "Okay," he began, "the Varginha Fire Department received a telephone call at around 8:30 AM on the morning of January 20th. Now, there are major differences between the fire departments in Brazil and the United States. The function of the fire department in the United States has solely to do with all aspects of fire, from prevention to actually fighting fires. In addition, the U.S. has an investigative branch that deals with arson, and another segment that renders emergency medical treatment. The United States version is strictly civilian in its operation and jurisdiction, whereas in Brazil the fire departments are actual branches of the military. Just as the U.S. has military branches consisting of the Army, Marines, Navy, Air Force and Coastguard, Brazil considers the Fire Department another one of it's military branches. Thire duties involve more than just putting out fires. The local fire brigade might be called to capture a wild animal, serve to combat a flood, corral a mad dog, or even capture a dangerous snake. The Varginha Fire Department has about 6 firemen who work within a local geographical area. They have a host of equipment, including the usual fire trucks, earthmovers, boats, and a host of equipment for dealing with wild animals such as nets, nooses, and traps. So with that in mind, the message of this early phone call was to report that a wild animal had been spotted near a wooded area in the Jardim Andere district."

I interrupted and asked, "Do you know who made the telephone call to the Fire Department?"

This fact is unknown," he replied. "But the response was to send four firemen in a truck. When they arrived on the scene they found five civilians: a man, a woman, and three boys, 12 to 14 years of age. They were just casually walking by the area when they noticed a strange creature going down a steep embankment and heading into a densely wooded area. Boys being boys, they began to throw stones at the creature to see what kind of a reaction they could elicit. Fortunately, the woman made them stop their activity. They stated there was no reaction from the creature and it just continued on its course. The fireman advised the five individuals to leave the area at once and they complied without question, considering the possibility that the creature could be dangerous. The fire personnel then went down the embankment and crossed over a set of railroad tracks, entering the woods in search of the creature.

The military crossed these railroad tracks chasing the alien
being into a grove of trees.

The city of Varginha has a very hilly type of terrain with a number of valley areas in between. The distance to the forested area from where they had parked their truck was about 100 meters. The embankment itself is very steep, dropping about 50 meters, and a ragged path courses down the length of it. Near the bottom is a railroad cut. The path is so steep it caused the firemen to slip and slide as they proceeded down to the tracks below. Once at the bottom they had to scramble about five meters up the other side of the cut. The path then continues through an old fence and enters the woods. The path is a treacherous one and returning is even more of a struggle, especially if one is carrying anything with them."

My interest was now peaked because this was beginning to sound like something one would see in a movie. Also, I began to wonder if there was a second strange creature involved.

Bira continued: "It took the firemen about two hours to finally capture the creature. It has been said the creature, once cornered, gave little resistance and seemed to be dizzy. Some of this delay was due to the fact it kept running away from them and hiding in the dense underbrush. Another factor regarding how long it took was that they did not know what this creature was and considered the distinct possibility that it could be quite dangerous. During the search, one of the firemen returned to his truck and radioed his commanding officer. He brought him up-to-date on the details and asked if he would immediately come to the scene. By the time the commander arrived they had already captured the creature and transported him up the long hill. It has been reported that a Major Maciel coordinated the entire affair. It was at this point that an Army vehicle arrived on the scene, accompanied by an Army truck with two Army officers and a sergeant. It is assumed that the commander of the Fire Brigade notified the Army. The strange creature was placed in a wooden box, which was covered by a tarpaulin, and loaded on to the Army truck, guarded by two armed soldiers. The truck then proceeded to ASA, the Army Sergeants Camp in Tres Coracoes, while the fire department vehicle returned to its quarters."

Bira stopped and studied our reactions for a moment before continuing. "There are more witnesses to the event," he said, knowing that I'd be eager to seek them out. "From a distance of about 100 meters, a number of brick-layers and hod carriers were working on a cement slab. They also followed the movements of the military vehicles. The adults and children who were the original witnesses to the scene had a discussion with a bricklayer by the name of Henrique Jose de Souza. He asked them what all the military activity was about and was told they were there to capture a very strange creature. Later, after the events, two military men assured me that this creature was being kept in captivity in ESA for at least 24 hours. They stated it was then placed in a cage, loaded on to a helicopter, and flown to Brasalia. From there, a United States Military jet took it to the USA. This is a fact, but due to the circumstances it cannot be fully verified."

Because we suddenly had more witnesses, and a new event, I asked Bira if there were others beyond those mentioned that he had not told us about yet.

"There are at least three more people who saw what was going on that day," he said with quiet confidence. "When all this was happening with the military and fire department, there was a construction project across the street. A new home was being constructed and a number of workers were on the roof performing their craft. I interviewed three of these workers and they told me they witnessed the arrival of the fire truck and corresponding personnel from the local fire brigade. They told me their attention was drawn to the firemen because they were concerned about a fire in the area that could prove dangerous to their position and the structure they were working on at the time. They were surprised to see the firefighters scrambling down the steep embankment carrying several pieces of equipment. They also described the terrain as steep and difficult to traverse. They stated the fire personnel were struggling, slipping and sliding as they made their way down the embankment. They then noticed movement in the adjoining field across the railroad tracks. At first they could not see what was causing this movement and thought there might be some sort of wild creature. They thought this was perhaps the reason for the entire episode. When they saw one of the firemen enter directly into the field they noticed something stand erect and thought perhaps it was a child who was injured. This would then have been a rescue attempt.

Hillside where the military searched for one of the Ets.

Their minds were abruptly changed when they saw the creature begin to move slowly toward the wooded area beyond and adjoining the vacant field. What they described was an upright bipedal creature about five feet in height with shiny, brown-colored skin. They stated it had a rather large head, and when it turned to look back at the pursuing fireman, they were able to see it had large red eyes. They also stated there were three bumps on top of its head. At that point they thought some animal had escaped from the local zoo and the fire brigade was called out to capture and bring it back. The construction workers told me that after both the creature and pursuing firemen entered into the wooded area they could no longer tell what was going on. They were able to hear voices, but could not understand what the shouting was about. Also heard were the sounds of crushing and thrashing in the brush. They also told me about the arrival of the military unit and their vehicles. The construction crew continued to watch and witnessed the firemen bring the creature out from the wooded area, carry it up the hill and turn it over to the Army unit, who then loaded it into a wooden box which was on the bed of a flatbed truck. They described the military people covering the cargo area of the truck with canvas. Then both the military and fire personnel dispersed just as if nothing had taken place. The workers then continued on with their construction activities for the remainder of the day.

"Bira," I asked, "how reliable do you consider these individuals to be?"

Without hesitation he said, "I consider them to be very credible and think they would have no reason for fabricating such a story. And remember, these people were totally unaware of other events that had occurred relating to the case."

Not wanting to waste any time, I asked Bira if it would be possible to visit the area where this activity occurred. He told me there was a current construction project going on, but we could still go there and see the exact field and forest. He then suggested we have a quick lunch and head directly to the spot. Phil and I both agreed, so we quickly dismantled the camera equipment and packed it into Bira's car.

Visiting the Site

After a fine Brazilian lunch we headed directly to the area Bira had previously described. As with the majority of other areas we had seen in Varginha, this was another hilly residential area of modest income housing. A mixture of what appeared to be older housing combined with numerous newly constructed homes lined the streets. One of the interesting points about these homes was that the newly constructed ones were architecturally the same as the older buildings; it was if someone had dictated a formula for building houses and this was the only formula available. In addition, even the color combinations matched the older constructs.

We proceeded up one gentle hill and down the next, finally coming to a stop across the street from a construction site. From where the car was parked we could see very little beyond the building project. We departed our vehicle with cameras in hand and followed Bira and Rudolfo to an area where a newly constructed deck jutted out from the street over a shallow precipice. At first I was a bit reticent to follow, as it seemed to me there was no guarantee of the safety of the structure we were about to walk on. The wood seemed new, but a supporting foundation was not evident. As we proceeded I could see between the boards an apparent sturdy array of beams and footings below. This gave me a bit more courage to continue our trek. Once we were almost to the end of this flat wooden overhang, Bira stopped and gestured downhill, explaining that the area he was pointing to was the little field with the railroad tracks and the adjoining woods previously described. At this point I was extremely gratified, as my mental concept of Bira's description did not match what I was now viewing. The area where all these events happened was far smaller than I thought. I had mentally pictured a very deep valley with a field perhaps one half mile across, but in actuality the valley I was looking at was only as big as an average residential lot in the U.S. The woods consisted of only several hundred feet of short trees entangled with a large amount of undergrowth. I could also see why witnesses to the event would have not been able to see what was happening in the wooded area. This was due to the dense ground cover and darkness produced by the trees. At the side of this wooden overhang was another level, constructed about two feet higher than the platform we were standing on. Bira suggested we climb to that level to get better photographs of the valley, field and railroad tracks below. Although the higher construct was only slightly higher than the level we were on, I found it difficult to navigate the flimsy plywood ramp temporarily placed there for this purpose by the workmen. I passed most of the camera equipment to my companions and proceeded up the ramp to the next highest level. When I finally arrived there I had immediate mental reservations about the return trek. We again followed Bira and Rudolfo out to the open end of this higher, man-made precipice. There was no guardrail or safety railing, which did little to insure my concept of safety. We then found ourselves looking over a precipice where the bottom appeared to be several hundred feet below. We quickly unpacked the camera equipment and began to photograph the scene. During this section of filming we listened again as Rudolfo reiterated the events that occurred in this area; this allowed us to capture his voice explaining exactly what had happened on video. Two still cameras were also used to record the visual images of this area.

We concluded our photographic session, gathered our equipment and left our rather precarious perch, heading to the level below; and finally back to where we had parked. Once there, Bira pointed across the street to a newer looking small house and told us this was the very house where the roofers were working when they saw both the fire department and the military activities. It made little sense to use the video for recording a stationary building, so we decided to only use still photography for this image.

We left the area and proceeded back to the Institute to make further plans for the day. It was about 3:00 PM in the afternoon when we arrived. Bira excused himself and told us there were a number of telephone calls he had to make. He also informed us there were several local UFO researchers who were coming over and wanted to meet me. Phil and I took this time to relax and talk informally. We found our conversation with the researchers to be informative and fascinating. We also took this time to draw up a strategy for the following day. It was our plan to visit some of the other areas around Varginha involving the case, including a quick look at the Varginha Fire Brigade. We also would continue the interview with Bira and talk about the next related event.

Discussion

It should be noted that there is no lack of eyewitness testimony in this case and this investigator could not determine the complete validity of all the testimony. In the end, I had to trust the opinion of those who did the interviews in instances where I was not able. Also, I did not interview the witnesses involved in this particular event for two good reasons. The first, because I was running short on time, and the second was due to the fact that many of them were not available.

The story of this event involves two main branches of the Brazilian military: the Army and the Fire Department. All testimony confirms both of these military branches worked together to achieve their goal of capturing what would seem to be an unusual bipedal creature. In addition, it is important to note that the description of the being matches both the testimony of the three young girls, Katia, Valquiria and Liliane, and the medical witnesses I personally interviewed at the hospital. Another point of importance has to do with the fact of geographic proximity. First, the creature seen in the afternoon by the girls was only a short distance from where the two military police officers captured the injured being who was transported to the hospital. This event, which occurred early in the morning of the same day, was also within reasonable geographic proximity to the other encounter sights. One might speculate at this point if these creatures were somehow dropped off in a nearby area. Some perhaps with injuries and others who were not injured—all of which did not escape the attention of the some of the local residents. There is also the question of how the military or fire department originally knew about these creatures. Were there witnesses who Ubirajara did not interview who perhaps notified them?

Also of great importance is the behavior of the creatures themselves. There is *no* testimony suggesting these creatures tried to fend off their captors, as their actions did not indicate they were hostile. They gave seemingly little or no resistance, with the exception of the creature who ran away into the woods. The witnesses to the capture of the creature by the two military police officers also stated there was no opposition by the entity. Only one witness gave testimony, which occurred at a later date, that stated the creatures were able to make a sound similar to buzzing bees. This was the only testimony in which the being was said to produce verbal sounds of some sort. I would have to consider the medical testimony to be the most important in this regard, as I am sure the doctors would have told us if they heard these oral emanations. There is also other testimony having to do with an odor produced by the creatures. I was also unable to determine if this was just rumor or fact. No one I questioned, including Mr. Rodrigues and the medical personnel, gave any credence to this rumor. The odor was supposed to have been unpleasant, like the smell of moldy paper or ammonia. In a later chapter I will be making comparisons between this case and the U.S. Roswell events, which occurred in 1947, however, at this time it is important that emphasis be placed on eyewitness testimony relating to the creatures involved in the case.

Could we also possibly speculate at this point why and how the military became involved in this case? Why is it, that in a small town such as Varginha, there was so much activity involving the Brazilian military? Why didn't the civilian population become more involved than they did? Were they too afraid of the unknown creatures to become more involved? These and many more questions come into play with few available answers. Perhaps the military was involved because it was notified some time in advance before actual events took place. It has been said that NORAD (North American Aerospace Defense Command) notified the Brazilian military that an object coming from space was going to impact in Brazil and gave them the exact co-ordinates and time of arrival. The events that followed would indicate there is perhaps some validity to this story.

Chapter 8

THE VARGINHA CASE UNFOLDS

EVENT #4

The time we were spending in Varginha was beginning to fly by. Would there actually be enough time left to come up with more evidence giving support to this case, or would we be cut short in the process of discovery? This question began to weigh heavily on my mind. I knew we must make the most of the time we had left and that meant cramming more into the day than just the interviews with Bira. With the camera equipment ready to roll, we started the next round of interviews with Bira early in the morning the next day.

"Bira, where do we go from here? You have told us of certain events that occurred which make up the heart of the case. Are there more events you wish to describe?"

Bira's answer not only simplified plans for me, but also put my mind at ease as far as the time reference was concerned. He replied, "There are a couple more events I would like to tell you about that are important to the case. Some of these may confuse the issue, but I will leave it up to you to make your own judgments."

I requested, "Please start with the event you feel is most important following the sequence of what you had told us previously." He agreed to this and explained the following:

"This event occurred also on January 20th at 2:00 PM. A jogger, who is a civilian witness and previously in the military service, asked that his identity be kept secret based on the following story. The area where he was jogging was in the Santana district. He noticed at least seven military personnel, who he recognized as being part of the Army, wearing typical camouflage attire, carrying light automatic rifles and side arms, moving in unison along a railroad line. He saw them cross a small footbridge, entering into a large pasture area immediately south of the wooded area. The bridge is at the bottom of a long, sloping hill leading across the pasture to the railroad tracks and higher up to the street where the fire truck had parked earlier in the day. This also was the same wooded area where the creature had been captured previously. [This is the same area we personally visited and photographed earlier in the investigation.] The jogger had intended to take a shortcut across the bridge, but changed his mind because of the military activity. He stated the soldiers walked up the hill and began to inspect a small grove of trees near the railroad tracks, found nothing, and then moved back the way they had come, toward the larger wooded area. They then fanned out in what appeared to be a "V" formation. Next the jogger describes them entering the woods, which was so dense he could not see what they were doing. The witness then continued jogging and followed a path that took him eastward into a street that bisects the wooded area, heading toward the Santana district proper. A minute or two later he heard the metallic sound of three distinct gunshots— Pow! Pow! Pow!—as if from a rifle. He was shocked and became curious for he knew, by his previous experience in the military, that the distinct metallic sounds made by the rifle discharges were light automatic rifles used commonly by military units. He turned and began jogging back along the path he had just come from, three or four blocks to the street overlooking the wooded area. He noticed at this time the presence of an Army truck parked where it had not been before. This was almost in the same spot as where the fire truck had been previously parked earlier in the day. Next the witness saw the soldiers struggling up the steep embankment carrying two canvas-like bags over their shoulders. Two military personnel had one sack, and the other two shared the burden of the second one. The witness stated that one of the bags showed movement, like something was kicking inside of the sack. The other had no movement. He described the volume of the bags roughly equivalent to the size of the being captured by the fire department earlier the same day. When the four soldiers arrived back at their truck they heaved their burden into the truck, which contained other waiting military personnel. Once their burden was loaded they climbed into the vehicle and sped away. Neither the witnesses or the investigators knew for sure what was in the bags, but it stands to reason it would not take seven armed soldiers to capture a wild animal, especially when four unarmed firemen had captured an unusual creature in the same wooded area earlier the same day."

This witness seemed credible mainly because ex-military are more inclined to remain silent about events that could clearly be deemed sensitive or secret. Bira continued: "There is another witness in Campinas who was in the same military unit as the individuals involved in this search incident. This person said he had heard that one of the creatures was trying to help it's companion who was lying on the ground, apparently injured, when the soldiers approached to capture them. The two creatures then fled into the wooded area. What he postulated was that the entity might have shown an attack reaction sign against the approaching military personnel and unfortunately ended up being hit in the chest with the three rifle shots. One of the creatures was different from the others in that it had black fur covering its body. When asked if the creature could have been wearing some sort of garment that appeared to be black fur, the witness could not answer. Please know," added Bira, "that this witness's testimony could not be confirmed or denied by any of the other ufologists who had worked on the case."

Now here is where the count of the total number of creatures becomes confusing. If two bags contained two of the creatures, one alive and one dead, we would have the capture of at least three or four of these beings. Remember, we had the one who was seen by the three young girls, the creature that was brought into the hospital and treated, as well as the entity that was captured by the two military persons. Bira went on to state that all of this information arriving in a fragmented fashion makes it not 100% trustworthy. It would then be necessary to wait until he could obtain future military testimony.

In separate but perhaps related testimony by another unnamed witness, the following story was told:

"I saw military jets flying over the city. I believe they were F-5's. They didn't seem to be in a natural formation and it looked like they were in some sort of attack mode. A little later the same day I passed a wooded area and saw seven army soldiers. [Note: This was the same area where a creature of some kind was captured earlier in the day.] The soldiers were combing the area and were dressed in green campaign camouflage uniforms. There were also some that were in plain clothes. They walked in groups of two. I wasn't the only one to see this, there were others. The other witnesses just vanished. I think they were too intimidated to come forth again or perhaps they were being watched. These other witnesses said they also saw the jet planes and heard the sounds of three gunshots. They also saw the soldiers carrying the sacks and described movement in one of them. Some of these witnesses waited until the soldiers left the area and went back to the spot where all this happened, looking for anything they could find, but came back with nothing."

In researching material relative to this incident I was able to find another well-respected Brazilian UFO researcher, Claudeir Covo, who found a source that affirms a local farmer had killed one of the strange beings with a gun. Another witness described a large number of military people in plain clothes, tracking something in the Little Jardim Andere Woods area. He stated that one of these men shot an alien creature three times in the chest, killing it almost instantly. He described the weapon as a FAL (Fuzil de Artilharia Leve or Light Artillery Rifle). Mr. Covo asks very provocative questions: What right do human beings, either civilian or military, have to murder alien beings? What is foreseen in the Brazilian Constitution? What about other country's legislation? Looking at the religious aspect, what about God's Laws or the Ten Commandments?

It might be interesting to ask, at this point, the following question: Who believes in the Varginha ET (or ETs)? It seems there is an available answer. Jo'o Ubirajara Nogueira, engineer and owner of the "La Neve" ice cream shop located in the center of Varginha's downtown area, organized a poll between February and April, 1996 with the following question: "Do you believe in the Varginha ET?" In this survey, 1950 people were interviewed, upon which 1530 people answered, "Yes", they believe in the ET hypothesis. 330 said "No" and 50 could not render an opinion. What this poll showed was that 80% of the population of Varginha believe this event happened and involved creatures from another world.

Back to the interview, I asked Bira, "What is your role in the dissemination of information to the public?"

He said, "I only release information I consider to be credible, such as the information I and my colleagues investigated and stated to be factual—at least in our opinion."

There was also the problem of protecting sources. He told us, "There are many witnesses who did not want to be identified and if facts pertaining to the testimony of these witnesses were brought to the attention of the public, they would probably demand to know the names and sources. So, in order to protect and shield these people, I will only allow certain portions of testimony to be made public. There are also those who have access to knowledge of certain operations, which are restricted and highly classified. These sources must be carefully guarded. These precautions are always taken in regard to media interviews. The actual quantity of information available is much bigger than one would think, but it cannot be disclosed until all the investigations are completed. Many of the witnesses, both civilian and military, will not make themselves known to the public for fear of retaliation; this is with good reason because such things have taken place in the past."

The biggest stumbling block seems to be secrecy. Bira added, "Some of the most important evidence in this case involves the actual creatures themselves, who were carefully removed from the scene by the Army. Whoever was responsible for this operation wanted the researchers to learn absolutely nothing. It is clear at this point to assume that the captured extraterrestrials are no longer in South Minas Gerais, but were transferred elsewhere to places of maximum security."

" Bira, is there anything else you want to add in reference to this event or about the case in general?" I asked.

He responded, "There is no doubt that intelligent beings from somewhere else have found us. The impact will be very strong on the human race and we will have to be ready for it. We are not alone in the Universe. Perhaps all this will serve to have humans think more about how we treat each other and the care of the planet we live on. It is unavoidable that later on it will bring benefits to the entire population. We, the Brazilian UFO researchers, believe what we are revealing now will be a conscious re-conquest in relation to the possibility of intelligent life on other planets. No doubt about it!"

This statement by Ubirajara was quite profound and left me with the feeling that there might be other significant data pertaining to this event or the case in general. I searched Bira's data and came up with the following material quoted in his files from a variety of sources:

"The repercussion of the episode reached beyond the specialists in Ufological research. One of the most popular Brazilian television programs covered the subject numerous times in a three-week period, and the mayor of the city of Varginha has considered the possibility of holding an International Congress to highlight and discuss the events. He realized that before such a Congress would occur the UFO investigators would have to finish their investigation of the case. It has lasted four months so far, and points to the Army as the responsible organization—as the ones who captured and secluded the bodies of at least one or two alien beings from the Varginha area. In a report signed by at least ten different organizations, they have unveiled a REAL, top secret, complex operation involving military and civilian personnel, which resulted in the capture of unidentified biological creatures. These creatures, according to the involved organizations, were kept under close medical observation for some time and later removed from the city."

Discussion

In general, it would be safe to conclude that there are a number of similarities between this particular event and some of the other elements I have mentioned in this writing. First, the description of the creatures matches very closely the previous witness descriptions; because of this, there is immediate and profound strength added to the case. The only exception would be of the being with "thick dark fur". It is possible that the "dark fur" represents some item of clothing worn by one of the entities. The next element in the order of importance is the geographic location of this event. It is in the same exact area where a previous event occurred earlier the same day and also close to where the girls had their original sighting. Other items also noteworthy involve the Army. It appears they were the major force involved with the capture and disposal of the entities, with the fire department only playing a minor role. Also, I have the feeling that their participation was something other than ordinary in relation to their training or military procedures. It would appear that many of the activities were not planned, and the participants developed procedures on the spot. We can only guess what events actually did occur that would necessitate the shooting of one of the entities, as the eyewitness testimony presented little explanation. Perhaps there could be similarities to the United States' Roswell incident of 1947, where testimony tells us there was one military person who, when confronted by one of the beings at the crash site, was repulsed by its sight. He allegedly called it a freak of nature, then hit it on the head with the butt of his rifle. We can speculate there is also a possibility that one or more of the soldiers perceived some action by the creatures' as aggressive and presented a possible danger, thus decided to shoot for purposes of self-defense. There is also the possibility of communication occurring, not heard by the witnesses, between the military personnel in the field and some higher authority during the pursuit, who ordered them to fire upon the creature.

We must also take into consideration the description by the eyewitnesses who saw the soldiers leaving the wooded area carrying cloth-type sacks containing unknown cargo. The UFO investigators all surmised that the contents of these bags did indeed contain the two creatures, one possibly alive and one deceased. However there is no direct testimony, from anyone who saw the military personnel, that beings were loaded into or emptied from said bags. Therefore, we can only surmise that the contents were the two beings who had been pursued earlier in the event. Could it be possible that the shots fired were done so to kill some wild species of terrestrial animal that might have been a danger to the non-earthly creatures—thus saving them from an untimely death on this planet—and that the more mundane cargo was the actual burden carried up the hill? Perhaps the pursued entities escaped and were possibly captured at a later date, or were never taken into custody at all.

In addition, it would seem there is no testimony to date to verify the direction or destination of the military vehicles that removed their prey from the wooded field. Perhaps again, at a later date, some military testimony will either confirm or deny these witnessed events. Since the case is ongoing and Bira's team is actively pursuing additional eyewitnesses, more evidence will be presented to shed light on not only this event, but the others as well.

Chapter 9

THE VARGINHA CASE UNFOLDS

EVENT #5

Bira had discussed the Varginha Fire Department many times and noted its involvement with this case. I felt obligated to attempt to go there and find out for myself if there is any obtainable evidence. Again, time was an important factor at this stage, as our time allotted for this investigation was rapidly running out. In order to make the most of the day we would leave immediately to get a look at the fire department facility.

Bira warned us again about the Federal Brazilian laws governing the function of the local fire departments in his country. He told us the facility was essentially a military operation and civilians were not allowed on the premises. He warned us that photography was forbidden and this included the photographing of the facility from the outside. After listening to this, I became terrified by even the thought of going there. I had not wanted to wind up in a Brazilian prison for violating some of their simple regulations. I asked Bira if he thought it was safe to even go there and he reassured me that his contacts locally made it quite safe. My friend Phil heard of the possible danger involved in this mission and was exhilarated and anxious to go. He is the sort of person who becomes thrilled at the thought of danger. In fact, it was not too many years ago when he had heard there was going to be an imminent hurricane in Brownsville, Texas and talked his wife into actually getting on a plane and going there to witness first-hand what a hurricane felt like. When he related this story to me, I was in a complete state of disbelief. Their adventure there proved more dangerous than he anticipated and almost cost them their lives.

With cameras loaded into Bira's car, Phil, Rudolfo and myself left to experience the Varginha Fire Department. From Bira's Institute the ride only took us about fifteen minutes. We passed through the downtown area and turned onto a narrow side street; this was mainly a residential area with a few scattered businesses. I was surprised about the location, as I had pictured something quite different—something more like a large military compound with high chain-link fences and guards at a gate. Bira edged the car over to the curb and slowed to a stop. He stated, "There it is—right over there."

He pointed to the opposite side of the street to a small, one-story building with a stucco exterior. There was an opening that looked like a garage bay and it seemed more like an auto repair shop than a Fire Department belonging to the Federal Government. Bira told us it was safe to get the cameras out and start filming the front of the facility. I did not understand this because of his previous warnings and was filled with trepidation. I asked him about this upon which he turned in his seat, smiled from ear to ear, and stated:

"Well, my friend, what I told you previously is true. What I am going to do is get out of the car and walk over to the fire station. There is no law saying you can't film *me*, is there?" We finally understood his meaning so we broke out the cameras and started filming. Bira exited the vehicle and walked across the street, heading to the front of the facility. We kept the cameras rolling and of course were able to cover the entire front of the building. Our ability to use the zoom feature also came in handy, as we were able to also photograph the signs posted on the building. We watched as Bira approached the open garage bay. Two fire personnel appeared in the open doorway and observed Bira getting closer. To my surprise, we witnessed a very hardy handshake ceremony take place. They were all smiling and their mood seemed extremely friendly. I watched closely through the lens of the camera. Bira pointed to us and waved indicating we should exit the vehicle and come across the street. I accepted that as an open invitation. We left the vehicle, still holding the camera equipment over our shoulders and crossed the street. A brief conversation took place between Bira, Rudolfo, and the firemen. Rudolfo explained to us that the fire department had heard from the mayor about my visit to the area and told them we might be stopping by to pay them a visit. I was shocked. So, I thought to myself—the hell with Brazilian Federal law. I guess the local authority takes precedence in this case.

We were introduced to the two firemen and they came forth with a friendly greeting. They told us they were happy to have us there for a visit and offered to show us around the facility. I was not able to understand their descriptions except through the interpretation of Rudolfo, but could easily tell there was great pride in what they had to say. I asked them if they were aware of the events of January the 20th, 1996. They responded by telling us they were acutely aware of what happened and were anxious to tell us what they could. They asked us to follow them to another part of the station that housed a fire truck. It was a magnificent site. There, standing before me was a mighty, bright red fire engine, probably of '60's vintage in absolutely pristine condition. Its height towered above me and its hood seemed the length of a locomotive. The fire personnel asked if I wanted to sit in the cab. I answered by hoisting myself up to that level, and took my place behind the huge steering wheel. It was like stepping back into time. I sat there thinking of how many times this vehicle saw active duty and imagined myself present during those times. Once the daydream ended, I swung myself back to the concrete below and into reality. I asked the firemen if they knew what happened to the vehicle used in 1996 for the capture of the creatures. They told me the vehicle I was just sitting in was the very same fire truck. I was stunned. At this point I could not resist asking them if they knew more about the case. They told me they were not present at the time, but had been at this facility since the day the original fire crew had been transferred. They also were able to tell me that they knew the six firemen who were present during the time of the incident in 1996 and still had contact with them and their families. I asked Bira to take careful note of this, as I considered this to be an important lead for future witness interviews. I knew we would not have the time to actually look up these witnesses during my visit, but thought he could continue this as part of his investigation at a later date. I could tell he was very excited by this prospect.

Next we were taken on a complete tour of the fire station. They showed us a multitude of equipment, including a boat with spare motors, rescue equipment, fire gear for high temperature fire fighting, external portable lighting rigs, ladders, ropes of all sorts and sizes, and communications gear. I asked them if they were aware of the story of the capture of one of the beings in 1996 when the firemen used a net to capture on of the creatures. They broke out in a hardy laugh and told us they did not use nets for that purpose. They gestured for us to follow them into another part of the building that housed other fire fighting materials. One of them reached up onto a shelf and brought down a long pole about ten feet in length. On the end of the pole was a metal loop apparatus and extending from this loop was a ring of cord. I could not tell if it was metal or rope but it did extend into a noose. The rope or cord then traversed the longitudinal axis of the pole. They told us this was the very instrument used in the capture of the creature I had referred to it earlier.

We received a complete lecture on the operation of this local fire department. One of the firemen came out with a yellow fire suit and asked us to feel the weight of the garment. I was amazed, as it was extremely heavy. They then asked us to don the gear, including helmets, which we gladly did to oblige. There we were—four yellow firemen. The flash of cameras sealed our fate, as we now had definitive proof of our visit to the Varginha Fire Department.

We had a quick lunch then headed back to the Institute to carry on with the interview session. This session was to discuss another one of the events surrounding the Varginha case. Bira explained that the event he was about to tell us about didn't occur until April 21st, 1996. It took place at 9:00 PM in the evening.

"Inside the local Varginha Zoo is a restaurant called Paiguerl Restaurant, which lies in the Zoo-Botanical woods area. This facility was available to be rented out for private parties. On this particular night one of these parties was taking place and was attended by numerous locals who were there essentially to have a recreational evening. One of the attendees was a lady by the name of Mrs. Terezinha Gall Clepf, age 67, who is the wife of a former politician and member of the Varginha town council, Mr. Marcos Clepf. During the course of the evening, Mrs. Clepf decided to smoke a cigarette and proceeded out on a porch-like extension of the restaurant so the smoke would not offend anyone at the gathering. The porch area was in total darkness. She looked to her left and was shocked to see a figure standing there, looking back at her. She stated the figure was about 4 meters away, and it was standing on sort of a parapet with only its neck and head visible to her. It was standing behind some railings that went around the porch area. This prevented her from seeing details of the body. There was no noise or sound coming from the creature. She new instantly it was not one of the ordinary animals confined to the zoo and became frozen in terror. She stated about five minutes went by and all the time she continued to stare at this creature without movement or gesture by either the creature or her. She described the being as similar to what was described by the three girls and the military several months earlier. She stated the entity had dark brown skin that was bright and oily, a rounded face, enormous red eyes which were slightly upturned at the outside areas. She described the eyes in much detail, stating they were emitting a type of luminescence, which allowed her to visualize the face in great detail. There were no apparent cheeks, no beard, mustache or visible nose and where the lips should have been was only a fine line or cut. The main difference between what she saw and what the three girls described was that this creature's head was adorned with what she described as a golden colored helmet. She assumed it covered the three protuberances on its head described by the girls. Still in a frightened state she re-entered the restaurant, remained totally silent, trying to regain her stability and coping with the emotional impact of the event. Once she had regained her composure she returned to the verandah and saw the creature still standing there. Desperate, she went back again into the restaurant and grabbed her husband by his arm, forcing him to accompany her out on to the porch. The entity had gone and she did not tell her husband of the event until later that evening when they were traveling home in the car. Mrs. Clepf was so close to the creature, her feeling of dread and horror remained for many months following the encounter."

Bira continued, "Twelve days following Mrs. Clepf's encounter another very strange event happened at the zoo. It seems five animals died of mysterious causes. These consisted of two deer, a tapir, a blue macaw and an ocelot. The biologists and director of the zoo, Dr. Leila Cabral, were shocked by this discovery and stated they have never encountered anything like it in the past. The veterinarian sent the entrails to Belo Horizonte for examination. A caustic substance was discovered in one of the deer tissues. None was found in any of the other animals. The exact reasons for their deaths were not determined. Dr. Marcos came to the conclusion that the entire episode was merely one of coincidence. This view was not shared by Dr. Leila, who decided these deaths had something to do with the strange creature seen by Mrs. Clepf."

I learned from Bira that his investigation uncovered the fact that Dr. Leila, in January of that year, during the time when all the attention was being given to the extraterrestrials in town, had met with a fireman and joked with him. She asked, "You captured an ET and guess who will wind up caring for him?"

The fireman stood there in a state of shock, his face ashen white. He turned to her and said, "Keep quiet and don't comment about this anymore to anyone. It is not something to joke about."

To this day there remains doubt and fear about the strange animal deaths. It has been postulated that perhaps these extraterrestrial beings may carry bacteria or viruses that are capable of contaminating and killing both humans and animals just a few days after exposure. Could this be a tangible reason for the military to hide the truth from the public? Perhaps if this knowledge were made public, it would result in a terrible panic. The answer to this question remains unknown.

Bira then related additional events following the zoo episode. "One night in May of that same year, a university student driving on the Varginha-Tres Coracoes highway saw a similar creature attempting to cross the highway. It appeared frightened and ran back into the bushes when it saw the car. The student was later taken back to the site where he had the encounter and realized it occurred at the very same place, right next to a farm, where the couple had seen a UFO in January of that year."

Another event, not related to any of the others, was then shared by Bira. "There is a Spanish UFO investigator named J.J. Benitez. In November of 1996 he infuriated a large number of Brazilian Ufologists when they discovered he had made a quick six-hour visit to Varginha. He unfortunately neglected to contact any of the original investigators on the case or any of the witnesses. He later stated he had found three holes in the ground in a pasture, in the woods near the crash site. He stated they were in a triangular pattern. Armed with this he went back to Sao Paulo and held a press conference stating he alone had found evidence of a UFO landing that brought the creatures to Varginha. This was something that none of the Brazilian researchers were able to do. I personally went to the site and found three holes in the ground in a pasture at the edge of the woods. They were spaced evenly, about 28 by 30 by 25 feet apart, over a steep area surrounded by more level patches, and were next to a tree described by Benitiz as being dead. I requested a physicist and agronomist to examine the three holes. Their conclusion, in a written report, was that two of the three holes had been dug by a post hole digger—with the excavated piles of dirt lying next to the holes, almost all washed away by the rains. The third hole turned out to be an anthill that had collapsed and sunk into the ground upon itself. Benitez had also stated he found desiccated insects inside the triangle formed by the holes. The fact of the matter is that there are numerous desiccated insects lying all over the pasture. The dead tree was very much alive in August and the third hole appeared much different than the other two. Also, the terrain for the supposed landing was undoubtedly the most impossible place in the entire area for a vehicle to land."

This ended the interview for the day. Since it was still fairly early, I asked Bira if we could drive to the zoo and film the area where all this had taken place. Bira and Rudolfo seemed excited about my suggestion and wholeheartedly agreed. We packed the equipment into the car and headed out to the Varginha Zoo.

The ride was only about twenty minutes. We found ourselves not far from the city proper, but in an area that could be mistaken for deep jungle. The foliage surrounding the zoo was thick and green. The roads leading into the interior of the zoo were paved but narrow, barely allowing one vehicle to pass another. Although the pace was slow, we were treated to a tour of the zoo by car, which in my past experience was not possible within the confines of the United States. Rudolfo supplied us with information pertaining to each area we passed and I assumed he had been there many times before. Since our main area of interest was where the event happened with Mrs. Clepf, our one and only stop was at the restaurant.

To my surprise what they were calling a restaurant was nothing more than a small elevated building that sat on a shallow hill. There was no sign of customers or other restaurant features. I assumed it had gone out of business between the time of the event with Mrs. Clepf and the present.

We parked and proceeded to unload the camera gear. From the area where we parked I could see a small paved pathway leading up to the building above. We walked along this path until we reached the top. The vegetation was green and thick. There was high moisture content in the air and collections of water droplets could be seen on the large leaves of many plants. I noticed an absence of flowered plants, and this struck me as rather odd but I assumed this was of natural design. There were a multitude of green plants twisted and entangled with each other. Soon we were on the very porch where the incident with Mrs. Clepf had taken place. Phil used the cameras, both still and video, to document our presence and illustrate the area. A friend of Bira's had joined us and offered to assist by assuming the position of the creature described by Mrs. Clepf. In order to do this he had to climb from the porch and walk around a narrow ledge above the road below. When he reached a point adjacent to the railing that wrapped around the wooden porch, he yelled for us to take his photograph. Bira indicated this was the exact spot where the entity had been standing. By doing this we were able to view the angle that the witness had of the creature. I could see quite clearly how she would not have been able to see the body of the creature at night without light.

We proceeded through the door of what had previously been the restaurant. The entire structure reminded me somewhat of a tree house. The building was constructed entirely of wood and had an odor of must and decay. I thought that perhaps this was typical of untreated wood structures in this part of the world.

When we finished filming we were taken to the area where some of the dead animals were found. The cages were empty and it appeared they had been unoccupied for many years. The thick foliage had grown into the rusty metallic structures and I could see that they were weathering at a rapid rate. Although we filmed this area, I was not convinced there was an important contribution that would come from the effort. There was a lack of physical evidence pertaining to what had happened to the animals in this area in 1996. Also, I could not foresee any additional data becoming available at this late date. The most I could say was that we were actually there on the very spot where these events took place.

This was the last area in the zoo we had to visit. It was now late in the day and fatigue was slowly creeping up on me. I longed for a hot shower and a good Brazilian meal. We left the zoo and headed back to the hotel. Plans were formulated for the last and final day in Varginha.

Discussion

Since I have become involved with the subject of Ufology, I have been exposed to a multitude of synchronistic events on a continuing basis. When

I decided to make this trip to Varginha I did not really have plan, but did have a goal of collecting physical evidence. A greeting from the mayor of the city heralded my arrival. From that point on it seemed doors began to open not only to myself, but to those who were helping me with the investigation.

Ubirajara, a respected attorney and resident of the city had numerous local connections. He had spent days, months and years investigating this and other UFO cases in Brazil, yet could it be possible that my visit opened doors that were previously closed to him? Could an indication of this have been our visit to the Varginha Fire Department? We went there with strong warnings that the premises were not only closed to the public but it was illegal to even photograph the front of the facility. I don't think Bira had any idea when we arrived there that we would be welcomed in with open arms. I believe my interviews with the medical personnel at the hospital, the wife of the deceased military police officer, and the fire department visit were not—planned or anticipated by Bira or his colleagues. The question then arises—why did this all happen? It began with the strange and unanticipated greeting from the mayor, leading to the other unexpected events such as our open and friendly reception at the fire department. Is it possible this was all part of some plan for me to get the word out to the public about the Varginha episode? Only time will tell.

One of the most important aspects of this case involves eyewitness evidence that can be corroborated. It is apparent that the description of the creatures fulfills this criterion. The eyewitness description of the entity by Mrs. Clepf matches very closely what we obtained from the medical personnel at the hospital as well the description of the three girls. This, coupled with military testimony, glues together a very solid description of the creatures. What is more mystifying is the time line. The accepted date of the original event was Jan. 20th, 1996. Months passed and more testimony has documented additional occurrences in April and May of the same year. Is it possible there were more creatures present in Varginha in January who escaped the attention of the military and then lingered all this time in some of the more desolate areas of the surrounding terrain? Of course if we accept the testimony of the medical officials who I interviewed, we should accept the fact that these creatures were highly intelligent. It could also have been possible that a rescue operation could have been attempted by the same species at a later date. Perhaps this would explain the time delay between the original encounter and the zoo event. It is a known fact that UFO activity in the Varginha area did not wane during this period of time. Prior to the January date, UFO activity was heavy in the area, which is a separate story in itself and was thoroughly investigated by the Brazilian researchers. There are many theories regarding this case which will probably not be resolved any time soon.

Chapter 10

THE CRASH

This was to be the final interview with Mr. Rodrigues, as the time I had allotted for the Varginha investigation was rapidly running out. I knew we had to conclude with any other events important in the case. I asked Bira if there were other witnesses we had not covered to date. He told me we had covered most of the witnesses pertaining to the creatures, but there were other witnesses, both military and civilian, who would not be available for me to interview in the short period of time I had left in Varginha. One of the important events we had not discussed was the actual crash of the object itself. He reassured me that the next on-camera interview would pertain to this event. I agreed it was one of the most important parts of this case and we should receive this information next.

Bira told us there were several witnesses to the crash landing of the vehicle. Some of the witnesses were in agreement as to the time and date of the incident, but others did not agree and their testimony was somewhat confusing.

One testimony came from an elderly couple, Orlina Augusta and Enrico Rodrigues, were working as farmhands. According to Bira, they reported seeing a UFO at approximately 1:00 AM on the morning of January 20th, 1996. This area of Varginha has been described as the coffee growing area and is all ranchlands. As they recounted the story, they explained they were both asleep in their house, which happens to be located adjacent to a road leading from Varginha to Tres Corocoes. The farm is exactly 10 kilometers (6 miles) northwest of Varginha, with their house located at the edge of the road.

Suddenly, they were brought to a rude awakening by the noise of bellowing cows. They jumped out of bed and ran to the window to see what was causing all the commotion. To their surprise they saw the animals in a state of total disorientation, running and darting back and forth, with some running around the outside of the house. Enrico was the first to look up into the sky and saw a grayish, elongated object slowly flying through the air over the field. He stated it looked like a flying submarine and was the size of a small bus. Orlina was next to see the object and she described it as slowly floating over the ground at a height of about 5 meters. She also stated that there was something like white smoke or vapor coming from the object. The both knew instantly that this was no ordinary aircraft or helicopter. They also described the object has having no lights and no motor noise. They stated it was absolutely silent and the apparently damaged structure had pieces of the fuselage hanging and swinging like clothes in the wind. They did not actually witness the crash, but realized the object was destined to do just that. The Brazilian researchers have pinpointed the time as having been somewhere between 1:00 AM and 5:00 AM, and have come to the conclusion that the ship had one of its ends damaged by an explosion, which scattered a large amount of small metal fragments around the region. They believe the ship remained in the air for some time. They have also postulated that because of the damage to the ship, some of its crew could have been dropped off adjacent to the woods near the Jardim Andere area and sought shelter there. It was also stated that an American civilian was present when the cigar-shaped UFO was loaded aboard a flatbed truck in the early morning of January 20th—a Saturday.

The Jardim Andere forest, located between the crash site and the outskirts of the park, is where the second being was spotted and captured later that day. One of the possible scenarios is that a number of these beings survived the crash and made their way through the woods, ending up in the park of Jardim Andere, six miles to the southeast. Some of the local residents have come to the conclusion that these beings were associated with the crash of a spaceship and were not seen until 7 hours later. There is also an unsubstantiated rumor that another farmer (not Rodrigues) shot one of the entities that crawled out of the cigar-shaped UFO.

Bira told us there was another individual, a college student by the name of Hildo Lucio Galdino, who told Vitorio Pacaccini (a well-respected and famous Brazilian UFO researcher) that he saw one of the aliens shortly after 8:00 AM that morning. Hildo opened his bathroom window and was astonished to see a creature with an oily, dark brown skin crouched in the alleyway. He described it as having very small hands with only three long fingers. It ran away when Hildo called out to it. He stated the creature wore no clothing, had no hair, and was between four and five feet in height.

When Bira had finished with this explanation, I was still filled with questions. I asked him if these were the only crash witnesses. He stated something to the affect that there were other witnesses, but their testimony could not be considered 100% factual. His reference was to several others who supposedly witnessed the crash. At this point I am going to present material that was *not* obtained from Mr. Ubirajara Rodrigues, but was verified by him as being factual.

The following material has been taken from an article in the MUFON UFO Journal, written by Bob Pratt and Cynthia Luce. Bob is a U.S. investigator who has, on many occasions, come to Brazil to perform investigative work in the UFO field. Several years ago he was presented with an award from Raphael Curry and A.J. Gevaerd for the best investigative research performed in Brazil by a foreign researcher. Cynthia Luce, an independent UFO researcher, lives in Brazil and has worked with Bob on many occasions.

Disclaimer

Much time has passed since this article was written. Ubirajara has stated that Souza has changed his mind in reference to the dates of the events and has come to the conclusion that this happened on January 20th. The following quote is from the original article:

"On Friday, January 12th, thirty five year-old Carlos da Souza drove across Sao Paulo, one of the largest cities in the world, and checked into a hotel in the northern suburb of Mairipora. He was going to Tres Coracoes, about one hundred and fifty miles to the north and wanted to get an early start the next morning.

Souza owned an exterminating business and his hobby is flying ultra light planes. He planned to meet other ultra light pilots in Tres Coracoes to arrange for a competition.

He awakened at four o'clock in the morning of Saturday, January 13th, got into his red pickup truck and headed north on the heavily traveled Fernao Dias highway (BR 381), which connects Sao Paulo to Belo Horizonte.

The drive was uneventful until about eight o'clock, when he was about three miles south of the intersection with MG 26, a state highway that leads to Varginha to the west and Tres Coracoes to the east. A muffled, roaring sound interrupted his thoughts and he wondered if something was wrong with his truck.

He stopped to check but when he stepped down from the cab, he realized the noise was coming from a cigar-shaped craft about four hundred feet in the air just west of the highway. The sun was reflecting off of it.

The craft was traveling north, almost parallel to the highway, at forty to fifty miles an hour. It was silver colored and appeared to be thirty to forty feet long, and twelve to fifteen feet wide.

It had at least four windows along the side and what looked like a big jagged hole four or five feet in diameter in the front. There was a long dent or crack running from the hole back to the middle of the craft, from which point white smoke or vapor was coming out.

Astonished and excited, Souza jumped in his pickup and followed the UFO for about ten miles. It soon crossed over to the east side of the highway and eventually passed over some small mountains. Then it went into a sharp thirty-degree dive and disappeared from sight.

Souza thought it has crashed and began looking for a way to get into the area. About twenty minutes later he found a dirt road and turned onto it. Minutes later he drove over the crest of a hill and there before him was wreckage spread over a hilly field of knee high grass. He also saw about forty soldiers and two male nurses, two trucks, a helicopter, an ambulance and three cars. All of the vehicles were Army vehicles.

Everyone was busily running around picking up pieces of debris. One truck already held a chunk half the size of a minivan. A strong smell of ammonia and ether hung in the air.

It was a terrible crash and Souza doubted that anyone had lived through it. He was surprised to see anyone there, let alone the military. He didn't know at the time that the site was only seven miles from the ESA Army base in Tres Coracoes.

He parked and walked toward the wreckage, thinking he could help. He picked up a piece of aluminum-like material that was very light. It floated to the ground when he dropped it.

Then one of the men spotted him, shouted and in an instant armed soldiers rushed toward him. They ordered him to leave immediately. He protested, thinking someone had been badly hurt or killed, but a corporal screamed at him to get out and that "this is none of your business".

Souza got back in his truck and drove away. He was so astounded by what he had seen that he abandoned his trip and headed back to Sao Paulo. About ten minutes later he stopped at a roadside restaurant to have coffee and think about what had happened.

The emotional impact was so great that he was still sitting there in his car two hours later when a car drove in with two men. They were in civilian clothes but military haircuts and bearings. One got out and walked up to him and asked if his name was Carlos da Souza. Then they asked what he had seen.

"I saw everything and know something happened there," Souza said.

"You haven't seen anything," the man replied, then related many details of Souza's personal life. "You live on such and such a road, in such and such a city. You're married to so and so, and you are the father of so many children, and your mother is so and so. If you tell people what you saw, it's going to be very bad for you. We already have a complete printout on your whole life."

Such personal information is readily available to authorities by computer once somebody's license number is known. The man warned Souza to not say anything to anybody, and then left.

All this occurred on January 13th, one week before the three women saw the creature in nearby Varginha, but for nine months Souza told no one except his wife and two close friends.

He explained he was frightened by the man's threat. A twenty-year military dictatorship had ended only a few years earlier and some of Souza's relatives "disappeared" during the dictatorship, so he kept quiet.

He was not aware of the "ETs" in Varginha until the following September when he read a magazine article written by Claudeir Covo, a Sao Paulo safety engineer and lifelong Ufologist who had been working with Ubirajara and Pacaccini.

Souza contacted Covo, who eventually persuaded him to return to Varginha to show him and Ubirajara where he had seen the wreckage.

An inspection of the area—now nine months later—showed no indication that a crash had occurred, nor was Ubirajara subsequently able to find any farmers, farm workers, or anyone else in the area that knew anything about a crash.

Not everyone believes Souza's story, and even Ubirajara and Covo (it was Covo who told us what Souza said) have reservations about it because no other witnesses could be found. Also, some elements of his story were similar to things that had been portrayed in the movie, *Roswell*.

In addition, Souza's description of the UFO was almost identical to one seen by a farm couple on the morning of January the 20th that investigators—and much of the public—had known about since early in the investigation.

Yet, on a later visit to the sight, Ubirajara and members of his UFO group found an area of ground about four hundred feet square that seemed to have been replaced with sod.

Furthermore, during the early stages of the investigation, several military witnesses said they had seen pieces of a crashed craft being transported into ESA by two Army trucks on January 13th and that later the wreckage was convoyed to the National Aerospace Center in Sao Jose dos Campos, near Sao Paulo.

"There are things that favored Souza's report," Ubirajara told us, "but we have to say that we could not verify it."

I chose this accounting of the Souza incident because it was most complete and, as I previously stated, there have only been a few new variants brought forth since the report had been written and they mainly have to do with the date.

There are many other rumors and undocumented testimonies that have been acquired by the researchers in this case, but to repeat them would lend little to the factual aspects of the case at this point.

Discussion

Since this was the last portion of the interview with Ubirajara, I decided to present it at the end of his other testimony. It goes without saying that this crash of a possible extraterrestrial vehicle actually initiated the case, but most of the emphasis has been placed on the survival and capture of the involved creatures.

Let's look at what we have in this regard—there are two testimonies involving a crash of some kind of a vehicle. One report confirms a date of January the 20th, which coincides with the other events, verified by multiple witnesses in the case, and another event supposedly occurring one week earlier with only one witness. We must also consider that this witness has changed his testimony so that it coincides with the accepted date of January the 20th. Is it possible he only did this to make his story more credible? Is it also possible he was telling the truth and there *was* an event that occurred on January the 13th? This would mean there were two crashes—not just one as previously thought. If this is the case and there were survivors, then perhaps it took them an entire week to make their way into Varginha proper, where they were seen and captured. We must also consider the facts pertaining to testimony of other eyewitnesses describing UFO activity in that area prior to any of these events.

Another scenario might lend itself to the possibility that the crash, known to occur on the 20th and witnessed by the farmer and his wife, was the only crash event. Could it have been possible that this craft had flown around the area for some hours, as long as it could maintain its airworthiness? During that time could it have dropped off some of these entities in order to save their lives? Some eyewitness testimony has described a UFO over the area of the Green River, which is wooded, secluded, and not that far from Varginha proper. This would have been an ideal place to drop off their crew for some measure of survival.

It is my hope that in the future some of these questions will be answered.

Chapter 11

LOOSE ENDS

Once the interviews were finished with Ubirajara and the pertinent witnesses, it was important for me to review the case from all available aspects. I believe the rumors were also informational and should be considered to some extent. The following material was obtained from numerous literature searches including some of the major web sites. These were written by a number of Brazilian researchers and will be quoted as such. The Varginha case is probably one of the most extensively covered incidents in modern Ufology. The number of sites on the Internet where information is available comes in all shapes, forms, and numbers, as well as in a variety of languages. I will attempt to present some of the aspects of the case, which are considered by me to be non-verifiable since I was not personally involved. These incidents and descriptions will not be in any specific order and are illustrated at random. These quotations involve many interpretations from Portuguese into English and may contain language, structure, and grammatical errors.

Number 1
"Since August of 1995, when humanity had knowledge of the autopsy of an alleged extraterrestrial, which sadly has been concluded by many to be a fraud, many were frightened by an increase in UFO occurrences where people from numerous countries sighted, photographed and videotaped many UFOs in the skies. There was a great world flap that still continues today and it leads to communication of these events through programs, both radio and television, to a large and ever growing audience. In Brazil, besides Varginha, there were several towns that reported not only sightings but also still photographs, films, landing reports, electromagnetic effects, sightings of beings, and even cases of people being attacked by strange creatures. Some of these areas include, Joacaba I, Santa Catarina, Sumare and neighboring towns in the interior of Sao Paulo. In addition, we have the coastline areas and the southern part of Minas Gerais, Guarabira in Paraiba and Manaus in Amazonas.

Some military sources, radar operators to be exact, confirmed there was an increase in the number of significative 'plots' on the radar screens in the last 13 months."

Number 2

"In the days preceding the facts occurring on January 20, 1996 in Varginha, many people saw several lights in the skies of that region. The Brazilian military secretly informed the Ufologists that the North American military were tracking these objects by the use of satellites and informed the Brazilian government of the great concentration of UFOs over the South of Minas Gerais. Without any doubts, CINDACTA I, in Brasilia, was also tracking these objects. Many military personnel were speaking about the military cooperation agreement between Brazil and the USA. [Note: These documents may be seen on my website, Alienscalpel.com.] The tracking by satellites allows the detection of the fall or landing of these craft within an error of a few meters.

By the action of the military in Varginha, there is no doubt that they knew in advance and anticipated what happened. Information was obtained in fragmented form but gave us an idea of how the military personnel acted so quickly. Probably CINDACTAI realized that a 'plot' disappeared from the radar screens. Their conclusion was, if it crashed or landed, where? The most likely answer: Varginha!; at least somewhere south of Minas Gerais. What was the nearest military base from that point? It was the ESA (Escola de Sargento das Armas) of the Army in Tres Coracoes, 27 km away from Varginha. A simple phone call and the entire operation started, under the coordination of the Servico de Inteligencia do Exercito (The Army Intelligence Service), known as S2."

Number 3

"On January 23, 1996 a Buffalo airplane left Canoas Air Force Base in Rio Grande do Sul. Inside it were three containers and many military people. In the first container there were generators, in the second the receiver equipment and computers, and in the third, a small workshop. In the box there was a disassembled antenna; in other words, a portable sophisticated radar system. The airplane went to the south of Minas Gerais. This radar must have been installed in some region or town near Varginha. At this time there were many alien ships flying over the region. Military people from within the ESA said that on a certain night they were worried about the hypothesis of retaliation from the extraterrestrials. At this time, several military people from the U.S. Army and Air Force arrived at ESA by helicopter. An area within the

ESA was interdicted. Several agents from the Intelligence Service (S2), and others from various points in the country were sent to the ESA. Local inhabitants of many years had never seen such activity in the ESA. That was something to call the attention of even the most naïve. If they were trying to hide something from the public, they failed in their methodology. The military people who took part in the operation, even today, are being observed and followed by the S2. Even today the situation is not good in the ESA. Recently, some of the military people from the ESA have said, 'Inside here, things are heating up.' They also said that if General Lima and Lieutenant Colonel Olimpio hear someone pronouncing the name "ET" or Pacaccini, they will get at least 10 days in jail."

Number 4

"On January 26, 1996 several NASA military officers arrived in UNI-CAMP. The official excuse was that they wanted to select Brazilian scientists to take part in future space missions with the Americans. Probably, they were military officers who know deeply the details about flying saucers and extraterrestrial beings. Military people said that the American military personnel were working together with the Brazilian military inside an underground laboratory. The proportion is fifty percent Brazilian and fifty percent American. Certainly, if there is a list with the names of the Brazilian scientists, those scientists will only travel in their dreams in the space shuttle. They will spend the rest of their lives thinking about the possibility."

Number 5

"On January 28, 1996 Mars Thereza Christina Strarace Magalhaes Texeira, wife of the deceased mayor of Campinas, Mr. Adlaberto Magalhaes Teixeira, was forbidden to enter the Hospital das Clinicas (HC) at UNI-CAMP, where her husband was when sick. She was very upset at the lack of organization of the local security scheme. With the help of a mobile phone she explained that she was the wife of the mayor and, upon the arrival of Dr. Otavio Rizzi Coelho, the problem was resolved and she was allowed inside. Some people believe that on this night the body of an extraterrestrial was sent to HC for some type of examination and the whole place was closed for security reasons, resulting in the confusion. Mrs. Thereza was only admitted because she was the mayor's wife. This did not occur with others who were prohibited from entering HC."

Number 6

"On March 1, 1996, the American Secretary of State, Warren Christopher, signed with the Brazilian Ministry of Foreign Relations, Felipe Lampreira, the "Agreement of Cooperation for the Pacific Use of External Space" [also available on my website, Alienscalpel.com]. A question hangs in the air: Would this have something to do with the Varginha case?"

Number 7

"On March 2, 1996, the general administrator of NASA, Daniel Goldin, visited the installations of the National Institute of Space Research, the INPE, and signed agreements of space cooperation between the two entities [available on Alienscalpel.com]. There had been such agreements in the past, but this was the first time that the principal director of NASA had come to Brazil to get to know the National Scientific display. People who are following the Varginha case, civil and military, believe that the presence of Daniel Goldin and Warren Christopher in Brazil involves agreements in relation to the beings captured in Varginha, and is also a form of justifying the presence of military staff who are active inside NASA at UNICAMP."

Number 8

"On May 8, 1996, ESA Commander, Brigadier General Sergio Pedro Coelho Lima held a press conference and read a clarifying note, saying that no element or material from Escola de Sargento das Armas had any connection with the facts being alleged. At the end, a reporter from EPTV asked him where the military people he cited were. He answered, 'Working for the Army and the nation.' The reporter answered back with, 'Can you prove that?' The general came right back with, 'Prove it to whom?' The reporter quickly retorted, 'To the press.' The general seemed a bit aggravated with the question and came back with, 'We don't have anything to prove and what I had to say was read in this note.' Thus, General Lima turned his back and left, leaving the reporters totally convinced that something rally strange had happened in Varginha."

Number 9

"On May 29, 1996, in absolute secrecy, for the first time in Brazil, a state minister met with the Armed Forces High Command outside the capital of the country. A historic fact! The Army Minister, Zenildo Zoroastro de Lucena, along with 29 generals, including the Armed Forces General Staff Chief, General Paulo Neves de Aquino and the chiefs of management and departments, including the eight military commanders of the area, met together in Campinas to carry out a task that could have easily been carried out by military people of lower rank. They visited the Escola Preparatoria de Cadetes do Exercito (Academy School for Army Cadets) to evaluate the EsPCex 2000 project, which is responsible for getting information into education, and for the creation of a modern teaching environment for the cadets, as well as a monitoring system for satellites. After this they visited the 28th Armored Infantry Battalion (BAB) to evaluate the 16 computers already acquired from a total of 26, which aim to create administrative procedures and assist in the the preparation of soldiers. So being, they went to EMBRA-PA (A Brazilian Research Center for agriculture and related subjects) to get to know the geographic information system. On the following day they went to the town of Pirassununga (Sao Paulo) to the second Regiment of Combat Vehicles, a unity of the 11th Armored Infantry Battalion, to accompany the work being done to receive 40 Leopard Combat Vehicles of German make, recently acquired. Military people from various places of the state of Sao Paulo, including the littoral, informed us that on the days before the visit of the Minister in Campinas, several meetings took place in Campinas, in Pirassununga, in Braganca Paulista, and probably also in other states, involving high ranking military people. They said that everyone wanted to go to Campinas to look at the strange creatures. Disagreements and misunderstandings even occurred between some of the military people."

Number 10
"On June 23, 1996, one of Ubirajara's friends from Varginha kindly provided his Seneca bi-motor airplane. During forty minutes they flew over the entire region, from the farm of Enrico and Oralina to the place where the strange creatures were captured. The main objective was to find out the UFO crash site. We were looking for a depression in the ground or a clearing in the undergrowth, or some burnt area. Unfortunately we had no success, but the photographic and video records remain available in this part of the research, and we are grateful to the owner of the airplane and his pilot."

Number 11
"On July 3, 1996 in the capital, Brasilia, the Congress approved a project that allows the Brazilian Air Force the power to shoot down hostile airplanes. The measure aims to give more power to the Air Force in its combat against narcotics traffic and contraband; being able to shoot down airplanes in clandestine flights that don't respond to identification orders. Of course, everyone is now asking what the Air Force will do if the target is a flying saucer. Certainly, because of former failures, the Air Force will often follow the target from a distance, only registering the fact in photos and videos."

Number 12
"Until the present moment, we have absolute certainty of the capture of two beings, confirmed by the military people who participated in the events. The possibility of there being at least two additional ETs is something we are

still researching, in the sense of finding military people who had participated in the events and may decide to collaborate with the ufologists under secrecy. If the military really did capture four beings (two of them were dead) and they were taken to UNICAMP, one of the living ones, according to reports, would have been taken to the USA. There is no news on the whereabouts of the last one, also captured alive. These beings are classified as Delta types. They are a species of trained animals and used by Alpha and Beta beings in more simple missions, as for collecting minerals and vegetables. They would be a species of Simian, of extraterrestrial origin, as well as being more intelligent than our Simians. The ufologists have classified them as EBEs—Extraterrestrial Biological Entities. As far as we know, until the present date, three beings were captured in Varginha with viscous skin and brown in color, and one with all the body covered with black fur (hair), including on top of the head. Both types have red eyes, big and bulgy.

To explain the great activity by the military people from ESA, it was said [by the military] that on that day they were greeting the new recruits, being that this occurred one week before. To explain the great movement of Army trucks in Varginha, it was said that the vehicles were envoyed to Automaco Enterprise to balance and align the wheels for driving, being that the vehicles were seen on Saturday and Sunday, a period in which Automaco is not working. To explain the great activity of military people in Regional Hospital, it was said that it happened because of the exhumation of the body of a young man who hung himself in the jail. According to the Exhumation Act, this happened on January the 30th, 1996, and the movements occurred between January 20th and 22nd. Nobody got to explain why the Army was accompanying the "exhumation". To explain the great activity of military people at Humanitas Hospital, it was said that this was because of the arrival of new equipment to be used in heart transplants. Well, it looks like a joke. What does military presence have to do with new equipment? To heart transplant an extraterrestrial? Only an idiot would buy that. Many declarations made to the press by Dr. Adilson Usier Leite, Director of Regional Hospital, one of the Humanitas Hospitals owners, leave a lot to explain. He insists in saying that the body of the person that was sent to Regional for exhumation came in a Fire Corps car. On the other hand, Captain Pedro Alvarenga, Commander of the 13th Fire Corps Company, insists on saying that they were not called to transport any such body. The Fire Department persists in saying they were not called to transport anything. It is time for Dr. Adilson and Mr. Alvarenga to sit down at the same table and come to some agreement. If not, the people of Varginha will end up suspecting that what arrived at the Regional Hospital in a coffin on top of a fire engine was really an extraterrestrial being, and not the body of a common human.

In conclusion, the Brazilian Ufologists have no doubt about what happened in Varginha. All that was described here is only part of the story. Many other facts will be discovered. It's only a matter of time, and the research continues today."

NOTE: Most of the above material was obtained verbatim from The Comprehensive Historical Report on Varginha *by Claudeir Covo, August, 1996.*

Number 13

The following was obtained from an article translated by Brazilian researcher Pedro Cunha, written by another brilliant and famous Brazilian researcher, Vitorio Pacaccini.

"The Varginha case is, without any doubt, the most important case in Brazilian Ufology and, possibly, worldwide. It started with the testifying of three girls that had a sighting, but already has reached proportions beyond this. Associated to the case, UFOs over the southern region of Minas Gerais state became more constant since a few days ago. We have conclusive witness evidence of sightings in four different towns, apart from each other by about 80 km. One of the witnesses is the mayor of Monsenhor Paulo. Because of these happenings, people from the region stayed alert and interested in everything that occurred.

From them, we had the opportunity to contact Fire Corps representatives, military police in Varginha, and Escola de Sargento das Armas (ESA = Sergeants Arms School) in Tres Coracoes, which increases the unnumbered details to the investigations, being possible to affirm with tranquility the truthfulness of the fact. It is extremely pleasant for me and for Ubirajara— the ufologist who commands the main investigation—to be able to be involved in this research. We always read and heard talks about the cover-up by the armed forces, but it is something distant to what is really happening in this case. We are here, living the facts and feeling on our skin the cover-ups that are being attempted and all the counter-information that the Army's Secret Service and the military police are releasing to disturb the investigations.

COMPLETE PROOF: We are feeling all the intimidation those authorities are exerting over the involved people in the operations and over the population. There are proofs that there exists an international intention to cover up the Varginha episode. This is not only a thing with Brazilian authorities, we have knowledge that in other countries it also occurs. But here it is in an extremely violent form. Even though we are fighting against those military forces—in the sense of taking the facts to the public—what has been valuable so far are the contacts we maintained with military people, which allowed us to find out how the capture of extraterrestrial beings occurred in Minas Gerais."

Number 14

The following is a quote from the late Graham Birdsall, owner and editor of *UFO Magazine* in the United Kingdom. He states:

"I had the good fortune to travel to Curitiba, Brazil and spend a week discussing among other topics, the Varginha incident with Mr. Pacaccini and several other leading researchers. Over 50 Brazilian UFO organizations were represented at a conference staged in the city between 6-9 June, attended by the likes of Stanton T. Friedman and John Carpenter.

Clearly, something of potential significance has occurred. Of that there is absolutely no doubt whatsoever. The Brazilian investigators have researched the case to the best of their ability (which contrary to popular myth is considerable) and accrued over 60+ first hand eyewitness accounts.

This was only made possible because they moved quicker than the authorities, and everyone involved in the case knew everyone else. Nurses, doctors and lawyers and significantly, several military personnel are on tape.

Let no one be under the slightest illusion that this is just another sensational story to come from Brazil. It most certainly is not. I was as skeptical as everyone else, until I spent hour upon hour listening to people who made me privy to some astonishing facts, the likes of which will become all apparent as further news begins to break about the incident (and there was more than one).

I've been involved in this subject since 1967, and I can vouch for the sincerity and credibility of those Brazilian researchers who have worked themselves into the ground to bring this case into the open.

My opinions are based on what I saw and heard in Brazil. I made a round-trip over ten thousand miles to meet these people, and listened with objectivity throughout. I returned to England with an abundance of information, and will happily disseminate as much as I can through the pages of *UFO Magazine* and at future lectures, beginning this weekend in Amsterdam where I will share a platform with Stanton T. Friedman.

Read yet again what Pacaccini has to say about this case, and digest every single word, and then perhaps the magnitude of what he and his colleagues have uncovered will strike a chord with those who have sat on the fence. This case above all others is set to explode."

Number 15

The following is a quote taken from an e-mail letter to Jeff Miller by Stanton T. Friedman, dated Sunday, June 30, 1996.

Jeff: "Yes, you may quote me. Based on my discussion down in Brazil I am satisfied that some very strange creatures were picked up by the government and that there were medical exams and military personnel involvement. Very likely there was a crash of something from space. Whether the beings were cargo or crew is another story. More investigation is going on. The case is very promising, but still in my gray basket. If more testimony is obtained because of the favorable news coverage, and despite the attitude of Friday's *Wall Street Journal*, it seems likely we will learn much more."

Number 16

I will now present two short stories that came to me while I was in Varginha. They are both anecdotal but have value in the overall consideration of the case.

It seems as though the wives of certain military officers had expected their husbands to come home for the weekend, as usual, since it was the custom to have these training officers only on base for five days per week. As with families all over the world, a number of these wives had made previous plans for the weekend involving their husbands. On the Monday following the weekend of the Varginha event, a number of these ladies also customarily reported to their favorite hair salon to have their hair done. As the story goes, they *did* make their appointments on Monday and complained bitterly to their hairdressers about their husbands. Their complaints centered on the fact that they all had made previous plans with their spouses for that weekend. Their plans were not fulfilled due to the fact that suddenly and without notice to them, their spouses did not come home as planned but instead, were out *chas - ing aliens* around the countryside.

In another story, it seems that one of the high-ranking military officers involved in the capture and transport of one of the aliens copied a secret videotape of one alien creature. He brought the video home and hid it with some other videos in their private collection. One of his daughters, a teenager, and her close friend happened to be home alone one evening when her parents decided to go out for the evening. As with all teenagers around the world, they decided to do something daring and exciting, so they decided to look for some porn tapes which they knew their father had secreted away in the video collection. They pulled out a tape and placed into the video play-back machine. What they saw sent them into a complete state of shock and horror, for what they were watching was the capture and autopsy of one of the Varginha extraterrestrials. Many efforts have been made to secure this video but so far, all efforts have not been successful.

Chapter 12

ROSWELL, U. S. A.—JULY, 1947
vs.
VARGINHA, BRAZIL—JANUARY, 1996

One might say that the July, 1947 headline reading, *U.S. Army Air Force Captures Flying Saucer*, picked up worldwide on the wire services, was the consummate **cannon shot** heard around the globe. This, of course, is in reference to the Roswell incident. We also must remember that in June of the very same year, Kenneth Arnold told of seeing flying craft that appeared like *saucers skipping over water*, hence the coining of the term "**flying saucer**".

It has been almost 60 years since this headline appeared about the Roswell incident, but even after this length of time it still remains the most significant historical case of its kind on record. Now comes 1996 and the Varginha, Brazil incident with far less international publicity—with small exceptions such as the article in the *Wall Street Journal*. Eight years have now passed and instead of the Varginha case fading into the UFO woodwork, it is gaining new momentum and interest. As of this writing, there is an impending UFO conference about to take place in Varginha, Brazil—the first of its kind in this area of the country. New information will be forthcoming from a large witness database. The Internet has now become active again with numerous opinions and ideas referring to this case. I will now compare the two cases in an orderly fashion, without being redundant.

Similarities
Some of the similarities are only superficial and of little importance, while others are more profound with greater meaning.

1. The Roswell case occurred in the month of July, while the Varginha case happened in the month of January. Both months coincidentally begin with the letter "J". Also, because of the difference between the northern and southern hemispheres, both months are in the summer season.

2. The Roswell case intimately involves the military establishment, with the U.S. Army Air Force taking the leading role. The Varginha case

127

also involves the military establishment, with the Brazilian Army and the Fire Department.

3. Both the Roswell incident and the Varginha case pertain to the crash of a suspected non-terrestrial vehicle containing possible alien life forms seen by multiple witnesses.

4. Both crash incidents occurred during nighttime hours.

5. Both incidents involve a hospital—Roswell with the Army Hospital located on the base, and Varginha with Hospital Regional and Humanitas hospital located within the city.

6. Both cases involve medical testimony, with Roswell witnesses from both the base hospital and a private funeral home director. This same type of medical testimony also occurred in the Varginha case, from numerous sources.

7. Both cases involve military transport of the craft, debris and bodies, with the exception that the Varginha situation includes the capture of live beings.

8. Both cases also involve the attempted suppression of eyewitness testimony by the military or some faction there of.

9. Both cases present an attempt to suppress the events that occurred by offering alternative explanations such as the "weather balloon" story in the Roswell case, and the story of the death of a deformed child in the Varginha case.

10. Both cases garnered global curiosity through the attention of the media.

11. Both cases involve the United States military.

Differences

There are probably as many noted differences between the two cases as there are similarities. The following are a few.

1. The Roswell incident involves the North American continent, while the Varginha case, the South American continent.

2. The Roswell incident seems to center more attention on the crash of a non-terrestrial vehicle with less emphasis placed on its occupants, while the Varginha case demonstrates the exact opposite.

3. In reference to the occupants, the Varginha case centers around the capture and transport of live beings, while the Roswell case places more emphasis on the transport of non-human corpses. Almost 60 years has passed since the inception of the Roswell incident. During that time, little or no testable physical evidence has been brought forth. Since it has

been only a short 8 years since the Varginha episode, there is a greater possibility of finding such testable evidence.

In the past, the United States Air Force has, by in large, adhered to their story of a downed weather balloon and seemingly will not come clean with the facts, however, there is a greater potential to get the truth from the Brazilian military.

Over the past several years, publicity given to the Roswell case has diminished, with the exception of last year's Sci-Fi Channel investigation, but more attention is now being drawn to new revelations in the Varginha case. At the time of this writing, a conference is about to convene in Varginha and new evidence will be forthcoming. The last chapter of this book, added at a later date, should contain the latest news.

4. Another very important difference between the two cases centers on the population of Brazil and its differences with those of us who reside in the U.S. It seems that we, as a society, are more easily intimidated than the residents of our southern neighbor. The Brazilians pride themselves on friendliness and openness. It is much harder for them to keep a secret.

The Brazilians have a long history of repressive government regimes and have learned to overcome their situations. Therefore, it is much more likely that information will be coming out of Varginha long before we can obtain the confessions we seek in the Roswell case.

5. The number of days involved in the Roswell incident is considerably shorter than that of the Varginha events, which continued to occur several months past the actual crash date.

6. The hospital involved in the Roswell case centers around a single military base hospital where in Varginha, two hospitals were involved, plus a first-aid station.

7. There is no evidence of any contact deaths from exposure to non-terrestrial beings in the Roswell situation, however, there is one suspected death of a military police officer attributed to contact with one of these beings in the Varginha case.

I could go on with further similarities and differences between the two cases, but the remaining written text of this book covers them in a more complete manner and you, as the reader, will be able to make up your own mind.

Chapter 13

DIVERSIFIED OPINION

Stanton T. Friedman wrote the following chapter at my request. I consider Mr. Friedman to be one of the world's leading researchers on the Roswell case. The opinions stated by Mr. Friedman do not in any way represent the author of this text, but it was felt that his overview has great merit in evaluating both the Roswell and Varginha cases.

Varginha and Roswell

By Stanton T. Friedman, Nuclear Physicist-Lecturer

Because I began the civilian investigation of the 1947 Roswell retrieval incident back in the 1970s, and am still working on that case, I am often asked about other stories of the retrieval of alien spacecraft and aliens at other times and places. By coincidence, I was invited to speak at a major UFO Conference in Curitiba, Brazil, in 1996, when I was informed, shortly before I left Canada, that a big story would be breaking at the conference. Not many details were given. Once in Curitiba, I heard the first public presentations about the Varginha case and was quite favorably impressed. I was offered the opportunity with the late Graham Birdsall, then the editor of the *UFO Magazine* of the U.K., and John Carpenter, a social worker from Springfield, Missouri, who has worked with over 100 UFO abductees, to interview Brazilian investigator Vitorio Pacaccini. He speaks excellent English and allowed us to film the interview with each of us asking questions. We also were able to hear a translation of much of the presentation of another investigator. Equally important we were allowed to view, and Graham was allowed to take a copy of, cartoon-like drawings of the buildings and the aliens, which were done partially based on interviews with the young girls who were important witnesses. John Carpenter was able to put together a 113-minute video documentary, "Aliens Captured in Brazil?" based on our interview and the drawings and the other discussions we were able to have, even though none of the three of us were able to speak Portuguese. Graham published a long detailed article in *UFO Magazine*.

131

Personally, I was very favorably impressed. There are differences and similarities between the Varginha and Roswell cases, as described, for example, in the book *Crash at Corona: The Definitive Study of the Roswell Incident*, written by Donald Berliner (an aviation-science writer) and myself.

Key problems with Roswell are:

1. That no one observed the downed craft in flight; the debris field was located near desert areas in the middle of nowhere; most of the original participants have died, many before I started the civilian investigation in the 1970s. Varginha, in contrast, is a large city of about 100,000 people and the crash was in a populated area, while Roswell is about 80 miles from the debris field. Most Varginha witnesses and participants are indeed still alive. There were some observations of a strange craft in the sky near Varginha.

2. Vary few civilians were originally involved with the Roswell incident, making it much easier for the government to cover up than in the case of Varginha. Military people were certainly involved in Varginha, but their ratio to civilians was much smaller. Several civilians saw the aliens from not very far away.

3. In contrast, with Varginha, we have no reports of aliens actively running around either the debris field site on the Foster Ranch in New Mexico, or the other crash locale, the Plains of San Augustine, over 100 miles west.

4. The small beings seen in Varginha were quite different with reddish color, oily skin, with seemingly small horns. The New Mexico aliens seem to be the more or less typical brown/gray beings with big heads, 4 fingers, almost no nose, mouth, lips or ears.

5. In both cases there is clear and definite indication of strong intimidation by the military of various people such as the medical personnel in Varginha and the rancher near Roswell and Grady Barnett over in the Plains.

It also seems to me that the U.S. government managed to get involved in the Brazilian case quite soon. It would be very useful to determine if the U.S. has offered a bounty for recovery of any wreckage of alien or Earthling origin that has reentered from space and landed in Brazil or other countries. Certainly our spy satellites are capable of monitoring the skies from above for peculiar events. Since for some years the Soviet Space Program was well advanced compared to the American program, any recovered satellite debris would be a great prize for back-engineering purposes and for evaluation of the Soviet state of the art. A case in point was the recovery operation conducted in northern Canada in January, 1978 of the nuclear reactor operated on board the Cosmos 954 satellite. U.S. recovery teams were on the spot very quickly. They were well aware that even back then the Soviets had operated at least a dozen space-based nuclear reactors to provide adequate electricity for such systems as side band radar for tracking ships on the ocean. All told, over the years the Soviets have operated about 3-dozen such systems whereas only one not very powerful U.S. nuclear reactor has been launched. It is of interest that despite the great public discussions in the media about Cosmos 954 and possible increased radiation to the caribou in the area, NONE of the media coverage focused on the very important defense aspects: that greater power would be available to the Soviets for better radar and for particle beam and laser weapons, which were certainly under consideration then to the Americans.

It should be noted that the U.S. government has had available to it as many as nine different teams of multi-talented people to follow up on any possible recovery of classified sophisticated nuclear, space or electronics systems anywhere in the world. These would include recovery from crashed airplanes and trucks, and objects from space. Obviously, one concern would be to assure that none of our advanced technological devices fall into the hands of our enemies or can cause damage (because of radioactivity, for example) to those near the area where the incident occurred. The other side of the coin applies as well. It is incumbent to recover any sophisticated equipment originating from other nations or outer space and to be able and to plumb the depths of its technology, whether foreign or truly alien, and to assure, as far as is possible, that interesting devices do not fall into the hands of other countries. It was the early recovery of a part of a rocket nozzle in Sweden during World War II that, upon examination by high tech "detectives", told us that the Germans were developing rockets, later identified as V-1 or V-2.

The work of such recovery teams would normally be conducted under high security. Obviously, the Cosmos 954 case was an exception since the public had been made aware that an orbiting Soviet satellite powered by a nuclear reactor might come hurtling down almost anywhere in a very wide range of places. Because I had done some work years earlier attempting to predict whether the Soviets would be able to launch such systems, I tried to get details about the reactor. The CIA claimed that such information was still classified. One might think the Russians hadn't known the details of their own systems. As it happened, I had predicted that they were doing all the research in many areas of technology that would have been required for the development of such systems. Even then the public was given cover stories indicating that the concern was with the radioactivity of some of the wreckage and the resulting possible exposure to northern mammals, rather than the high tech advantages of the system, whose technology was years ahead of ours.

The late Dr. John Mack, respected Harvard psychiatrist, interviewing Valquiria and Liliane.

An important aspect of the Varginha case to me was that Dr. John Mack, the courageous Harvard psychiatrist who has worked with a number of abductees, was able to interview the young girls who were the original witnesses using the services of an interpreter. It was John's conclusion that the girls were being truthful. There were no civilian investigators interviewing military or civilian personnel involved with Roswell in 1947.

A question that came up in Curitiba that I believe to be relevant regarding Varginha is whether the beings, whether crew or cargo, had gotten loose. There seemed to be no high tech gadgetry with them and they seemed very frightened of their immediate environment. Usually aliens seem to have things under control near sites where they have landed. Ted Phillips of Reeds Spring, Missouri, has, over the past 35 or more years, collected information about roughly 5000 physical trace cases from 75 countries.

In about 16% of these cases beings are observed near the craft hovering just above or sitting on or near the ground. Many of these cases have multiple witnesses. Tests have also been run on the soil beneath where the saucer had been, indicating permanent or almost permanent effects. In Delphos, Kansas, for example, the soil was dried out down 14 inches deep in a circular region, lifesaver shaped, about one foot across and ten feet in diameter. The effected ring soil would not support seed germination, nor would it absorb moisture, though control samples from nearby would do both. One possible explanation would be intense microwave exposure, perhaps from the power plant upon take off and/or landing.

At the debris field outside Roswell, no civilians were able to obtain samples of the soil immediately after the crash wreckage had come to rest. Similarly, we have no direct knowledge of the effects on the soil beneath where the almost intact saucer landed (crashed) over in the Plains of San Augustine at the same time.

The United States government has released absolutely no technical data on the wreckage that was retrieved, the beings that were recovered at both sites, or on the ground at either place. We do know that the area was carefully screened or reviewed, as though they had "vacuumed" the desert. Wreckage would have been the primary goal, but effects on the ground would also have been of great interest. Were chemicals spilled? Had high temperatures been present? Was the desert fauna or flora affected? Any cooked field mice?

If the Varginha beings were of a different species or from a different society, there would certainly have been great pressure to learn anything new that might be available about them and their craft. There was no DNA testing or a host of other sophisticated biological testing techniques available in 1947. These could easily have been used in Varginha. Think of all the new tests that have been done in connection with cold case, criminal crime scenes. Another case that illustrates intimidation of local people, secreting of wreckage, connections between local fire and police departments and the federal government is the Kecksburg, Pennsylvania, crash retrieval case, so well investigated by Stan Gordon of Pittsburgh. Journalist Leslie Kean has still not released government files despite legal efforts under the Freedom of Information Act and others connected with the Science Fiction Television Network.

One very interesting contrast between Roswell and Varginha is the involvement of the press. There were indeed front-page headline stories about the flying disc recovered near Roswell in American evening papers only, from Chicago west, on July 8, 1947. By the next day the cover story of a radar reflector weather balloon combination was splashed all around the world. It wasn't until 1997 that the U.S. Air Force admitted they had lied in 1947, by now claiming that the wreckage had been a Project Mogul balloon. That explanation doesn't fit either, but the press bought it. There had been almost no interviews with the Roswell cast of characters at the time. In contrast, the press in Brazil gave a great deal of reasonably accurate coverage to the Varginha incident. The girls were interviewed. The story was treated like any other major story, which helped to bring out more witnesses. There was essentially no TV coverage of the Roswell incident but quite a bit about Varginha.

In both cases there are probably still small pieces of wreckage not under government control. Pilot Pappy Henderson, who had been part of the 509th and had flown some of the wreckage to Wright Field from Roswell, had kept a small piece which he showed to close friends and family. He died in 1986 and we haven't been able to locate the piece. One can only hope that some pieces of what was recovered at Varginha will be made available and tested appropriately.

Undoubtedly there have been other crash retrieval events about which we know nothing. As an optimist, I am still looking for important witnesses to come forth.

Chapter 14

THE 2004 VARGINHA CONFERENCE

Before this work was completely finished, I was led to the to the discovery of new information pertinent to the Varginha case. Fortunately, I was able to obtain this information prior to publication here in the U.S. I have condensed it and now proudly present this information to you, the reader.

The first conference on the subject of UFOs was held in Varginha, Brazil, August 19th through August 22nd, 2004. This was the first conference of its kind held in this city. Unfortunately I was not present but I understand from my contacts in Brazil that it was well attended by some of the most important Brazilian UFO researchers and the public. Some extremely new and exciting information was presented. There was new testimony involving medical treatment given to the deceased military police officer and other pertinent data in general.

I would like to thank A.J. Gevaerd, Ubirajara Rodrigues, and my very dear friend Gildas Bourdais in France for supplying me with this material so that it could be included in this text. Originally, the material was presented in Portuguese and translated into French by Gildas, who was kind enough to translate it into English for me to use.

New Revelations
One of the physicians who treated the deceased military policeman who was involved with the contact and capture of the ET in Varginha offers new evidence.

The following interview is with Dr. Cesario Lincoln Furtado.
Source: *UFO Magazine Brazil*, No. 102.
All material supplied by A.J. Geveard, Ubirajra Franco Rodrigues, and Cesario Lincoln Furtado. Translation and summary by Gildas Bourdais.

"One of the most serious and appalling incidents that occurred in the Varginha case was the death of a military police officer on February 15, 1996. Corporal Marco Eli Chereze passed on at the young age of 23. Marcos was part of the Secret Service division of the military police. He participated in the capture of the second non-terrestrial creature on the night of January 20, 1996.

The news of his death spread swiftly during the first few months of the case and investigations. All that could be ascertained was that a military policeman had died because of a generalized infection after having been in direct contact with an alien being. Because of the gravity of the situation, the subject of his death was treated with extreme caution by the investigators. Meanwhile Ubirajara Rodrigues, a prominent Varginha attorney and consultant to the *UFO Review*, continued to search for new information about the case.

Rodrigues reviewed material from the local City Hall and found documentation stating that a policeman had expired after contact and capture of one of the creatures. He then obtained a copy of the death certificate and from that he located the family of the soldier. The same witness who alerted the investigators about the death of Chereze stated that during the capture of the being there was a moment of mild resistance, which forced Chereze to touch the entity on his left arm with bare hands. This is what they believe to be the cause of his infection. It was the opinion of some of his colleagues that he would have been contaminated 'one way or another.'

It is this author's opinion that if this same episode happened here in the United States, this death would never have happened. Through the years our teams have gained a genuine respect for non-terrestrial infective agents. One example is by the care we take in our space vehicle launches, making sure there is a safe and sterile environment housing the spacecraft.

After his death, Marco's family managed to have an inquiry opened by the local police precinct in order to establish eventual medical responsibilities for his death. At that time searches seemed to be doomed to failure, but continue till this day. It should be noted that a few days after his exposure to the being, a small tumor similar to a furuncle appeared in one of Marco's armpits. The tumor, according to what was learned at the time, would have usually been removed on the premises of where he was serving his duty. It was learned this did not happen. It was also noted that the family was alarmed because of the lack of information they received about Marco's condition and, later, his tragic death. Even months after his burial no one was told the exact cause of his death."

Autopsy Refused

"It was strange that the police superintendent himself, even after insistence, was not allowed to be present during the autopsy. The retention and dissemination of information regarding that subject is an affront to the family of

Chereze, and to the laws of the nation. A further affront was committed by the military police itself. It was one year after the event in Varginha, on January 20, 1997, that things began to move. This was due to the very strong movement publicly denouncing these past events by the ufologists and the press.

Among the most disquieting facts put forward by the investigators was precisely the absence of information regarding this untoward death. This became the Varginha case's worst headache. In the middle of a press conference, which occurred at the first anniversary of the event, the investigators denounced the silence by all involved and with that methodology in place, were successful in gaining access to the autopsy file. From its contents, it was determined that Chereze had expired from a generalized infection. They went on to learn that Marco arrived home after the night of the event, suffering from strong pain in his back. Once the small tumor had been removed from his armpit, he began to suffer a gradual paralysis and fever which became worse over a short period of time. He was then admitted to hospital Bom Pastor, where he remained confined and isolated from his family during the next several days.

Close relatives, especially his sister, Marta Antonia Tavares, was the one who most frequently visited the hospital and was refused contact with her brother. She also had great difficulty in contacting the doctor who was Marco's physician and in charge of the case. She was not given any information regarding his condition or what the diagnosis was. Only a short time passed before Cherese was transferred to hospital Regional Do Sul de Minas, located in Varginha. This is the same hospital where on the night of January 20th he brought the captured creature. Chereze was admitted to this hospital and placed in the center for intensive care. The physician in charge of his case at this facility has now come forth and will reveal what he knows about the case:

'Chereze passed away at 11:00 AM on February 15, 1996, twenty-six days after his exposure to an extraterrestrial being. Although all the tests and exams possible were applied to the search for a diagnosis, the patient could not be saved in time.'

This statement was made during a deposition before the judge of the 'COMARCA'. It was discovered that the physicians who took care of Chereze at the time did not have the faintest idea of how to treat the illness which was striking him down. After his death had been revealed, there was a meeting with the press in January, 1997. At this meeting the commander of the military police of the state of Minas Gerais vehemently denied the facts presented, including Cherese's activities on the night of January 20, 1996."

Another story was introduced that was absolutely absurd:

"The family of Marco Eli Chereze confirmed he was indeed on duty that night. Furthermore, he did not die from any of his professional activities after contact with the alien creature. It should be noted that the alien creature died in a much shorter time than Chereze. It seems clear that the circumstances of the death of the policeman has become the least controllable and most dangerous piece of the process of dissimulation imposed by the military of the ESA and the Brazilian Army".

The following is an interview with Dr. Cesario Lincoln Furtado, performed by Ubirajara Franco Rodrigues. Summarized by Gildas Bourdais.

Ubirajara Rodrigues asked Dr. Cesario Furtado what his role was in the treatment of the military policeman Chereze at the hospital facilities in Varginha. The following is the summary of his answers to several questions, condensed in chronological order:

Dr. Cesario: "Marco Eli Chereze was first admitted in the department 'Prontomed' (Emergency Room) of the Hospital Regional by my colleague Armando Martins Pinto (cardiologist) on February 12, 1996. He entered there because of an intense pain in the lumbar area. Dr Armando directed him to the hospital Bom Pastor where Dr. Rene rapidly took him in charge. He was a cardiologist, general practitioner, and head of the Department of Cardiology. He ordered some examinations to be performed. I then became involved, being that I was supervisor and coordinator of cardiology at Bom Pastor.

Questioned by Ubirajara, Dr. Cesario explained he worked in both hospitals, however, during that month, January of 1996, he was not supposed to be on duty at Hospital Regional. He was on duty every morning at Bom Pastor. The reason that Chereze was sent to Bom Pastor is not clear. Perhaps it was because of the lack of room at the Regional facility, or perhaps it had to do with his military coverage.

Dr. Cesario: "The next day at Hospital Bom Pastor we asked for new exams because the patient was still suffering discomfort in the lumbar area. We asked for urine analysis and x-rays of the spinal column in the lumbar and sacral areas. In addition, we ordered a consult from an orthopedist. The pain was so intense we suspected the presence of a herniated disc. Dr, Rogerio Lemos, in charge of orthopedics, examined him and told us there was no alteration and the symptoms did not originate from there. He advised us to continue our search for the cause of the pain. A fever began to appear shortly thereafter.

The blood analysis, which arrived in the afternoon, showed a leucocytosis, with a shift to the left and toxic granulations in the neutrophils. This was the sign of a serious infection highly capable of provoking a poisoning (toxemia)—because there were those toxic granulations. We then administered two antibiotics—penicillin and gentamycin—because we thought there could be pneumonia, owing to the localization of the pain or possibly a urinary infection.

His case was evaluated again on February 13th. The condition had stayed the same. The next day he was still at hospital Bom Pastor. He spent the day with fever and pains, but at an 'acceptable level' and remained at that level until the morning of the 15th, when he woke up very tired and in a state of torpor and signs of cyanosis. These symptoms seemed to confirm a general poisoning vehiculated by the blood, with a possible outcome of septicemia. He was then immediately transferred to the CTI (Intensive Care Unit) of Hospital Regional, where he was medicated.

At CTI of Hospital Regional, one of the first exams was for HIV infection, with a negative result. His state of health deteriorated rapidly and he died in a few hours, although he had been given antibiotics soon after his admission. This intrigued everyone and an autopsy was performed. It did not confirm a urinary infection but that was later confirmed by a urine culture, which had been ordered at hospital Bom Pastor. He also had a mild pneumonia." Dr. Cesario added, "In my opinion, the urinary infection was the cause of the septicemia because the pulmonary infection was so minimal that it could not have been responsible for such a state."

The close relatives of Chereze, mainly his sister Antonia, says Dr. Cesario suspected that the abscess Chereze had in his left armpit, after the military operation, was not properly treated and may have caused the infections. Dr. Cesario denies this because when Chereze was admitted to the hospital, the abscess was practically healed. Furthermore, the abscess was due to another bacteria, a staphylococcus, which is normal for any small, superficial infection of the skin.

The main point, insists Dr. Cesario, is that the cause of his death—the causa mortis—has not been clarified. A few days before the boy was in good health, and at the beginning, the infection looked relatively simple. He never had, in the past, any difficult treatment that could have caused an immunodeficiency. It could not be congenital either, because had this been the case he would have never reached 23 years of age in good health. This is why we can affirm that his immunodeficiency was "acquired" and we don't know how. His death was not caused by pneumonia, urinary infection, or by the abscess.

Dr. Cesario also went on to state: "At the beginning, the diagnosis of a urinary or kidney infection prevailed because of the presence of 'enterobacteria'. It is hard to believe that in less than twenty days three bacteria attacked the policeman. THREE! This is a very rare thing in this world. Marco had a pulmonary infection; he already had no immune defense. In that case, any bacteria can take control of a person".

At the request of Ubirajara, Dr. Cesario gives more medical details:

.

Dr. Cesario: "In the hemogram sent by the laboratory of Bom Pastor, it is said there is a presence of cytoplasmic vacuoles. The presence of 8% of thin, toxic granules in the neutrophils. Direct poikilocytosis".

Ubirajara asks: "How can you, as a physician, interpret the presence of 8% of those toxic granulations in the neutrophils?"

Dr. Cesario: "They appear in the neutrophils of a person who is the victim of aggression of very virulent bacteria. This provokes a 'battlefield', if we may say, which could reach 50% to 60%. The file mentions 8% because it refers to the first blood analysis. That demonstrates there is an infection, which led to the prescription for antibiotics. Their presence denotes an important and serious infection. It is not frequent except in serious cases".

Ubirajara: "In Ufological circles, some researchers will read this statement on the results of the hemogram, and are going to interpret that those 8% of toxic granulations were 'unknown things', the presence of a new substance, or something else".

Dr. Cesario: "No, nothing like that, absolutely nothing. As I said already, they don't appear normally in all infections but are frequent in serious infections."

Ubirajara: "During the time that you took care of the policeman, did you notice at the Bom Pastor or at Hospital Regional the presence of any unknown physicians, from outside?"

Dr. Cesario: "No, I did not notice any. I did not see either the superiors of Marco Eli Chereze, whether from the police or the army. They did not look for me, not even to collect the slightest amount of information regarding the boy during the two or three days."

Ubirajara: "There is, in the medical inquiry following Marco's death, the deposition of a dermatologist. He mentions a blood infection, in which red cells would have been attacked by white cells. According to this dermatologist, those 8% in the blood examination could have denoted a contagion by the skin of an eventual toxic substance, which would have attacked the red cells. What do you think of that?"

Dr. Cesario: "This has nothing to do with the anything. There is no connection between these elements. The report also says that a few days could have passed before the process materialized. If there were such a contagion by the skin, its effect would be blazing. We would be decimated every day that way."

Ubirajara: "Could you see the body?"

Dr. Cesario: "No, I could not. It is not usual. After death the body is taken for the autopsy and there is no other recourse. After a person is deceased, you inform the family. In the case in question, I was not even the person who did that, because when they took him to the CTI, I transferred my responsibilities to the other doctor at the CTI."

Ubirajara: "Did the family think of asking for an exhumation of the body?"

Dr. Cesario: "Not that I know of. In fact, an exhumation would not have brought proof of what really caused the death. As far as the death certificate goes, the cause of death was not mentioned because there was not the faintest element to guarantee anything."

Ubirajara: "You mentioned that a member of his family had affirmed that he wanted to know what this illness was about, because the policeman had participated in the capture of something strange. Was this told to you before or after his death?"

Dr. Cesario: "A few days later, when his death was still recent. I don't remember very well, but his sister was in great shock and she came to talk with me."

Ubirajara: "Lets stick to the facts regarding this interview. Did you notice any other movement at the time, in one of these hospitals?"

Dr. Cesario: "I heard of many things, but I did not witness any particular movement. However, rumors were thriving at the maternity ward of Hospital Regional, but I never worked there, not being an obstetrician. Furthermore, the maternity ward was somewhat separate, the entrance and the rest of it. As for the Hospital Humanitas, where I also worked at the time, I did not notice anything. There were not even comments between doctors, nurses, and office personnel."

Ubirajara went on to ask if there could be isolated areas of these hospitals. Dr. Cesario explained that at Regional, there was a reserved aisle, used for contagious patients. At the Humanitas there were few movements, and there were many rooms without activity. In 1996 there were no longer isolation premises, except in hospitals that specialized in contagious diseases.

Ubirajara: "Do you see other interesting aspects to mention about that episode?"

Dr. Cesario: "Listen, there is that story reported by the family (regarding the capture of the being) which I don't know anything about. But, we don't find any rational explanation for the death of this boy, because it was terribly fast, you understand?"

Ubirajara: "Could it have been caused by a completely unknown bacteria, however improbable?"

Dr. Cesario: "Yes! Well, if we talk of something completely unknown, it is obvious that we could not risk any conjectures. There is no answer possible. Now, could something have penetrated inside his organism, something equally unknown, which could have deprived him of his immunity system? This is another question without answer."

Ubirajara: "Could you tell what type of thing would be susceptible to provoke that, for instance?"

Dr. Cesario: "I don't know. That might be an injectable 'poison' or an infection of injured skin on the face or the foot. It might be an injury caused by a nail, which would provoke tetanus, etc. But we know how tetanus works. A multitude of things, I might say, and this is just to enumerate some of what might have contaminated that boy and deprived him of his immune resistance. I repeat that I say it "COULD BE".

Ubirajara: "Are you telling me that the death of Marco Eli Chereze was a strange death?"

Dr. Cesario: "A strange death, without rational explanation. In the course of my professional life, I have seen already two persons, age about 25, die of an infection, but we knew that both had immune deficiency. Both of them, if I recall well, had their spleen removed (splenectomy) following a past accident. After a certain delay, that causes immunodeficiency. In that situation, the person may die rapidly if they find themselves in the condition of septicemia. But, once again, it was not in this case."

Author's Comments

I have been involved in medical science now for 41 years. Each year, each month, and each day of practice I come across new problems that I was not exposed to previously. As time goes on, our understanding of human physiology and pathology expands. One of the most important comments I can make in reference to this case is that I was *not there* at the time when this individual was treated.

My investigation of this case has always been after the fact. My interview with the previous doctor illustrated in this text was slightly different than the session by Ubirajara. Bira did a terrific job as an attorney in bringing forth answers to his questions but unfortunately, as with most professions, we cannot know all subjects in detail. A mechanic could question a plumber and perform an adequate inquisition, but because his subject is so far afield from the plumber's, he would not know to ask the detailed questions necessary to adequately broaden the scope of his complete understanding. At this point I can only comment about Dr. Cesario's answers.

During my own investigation of this case, I amassed testimony from a number of different sources. The symptoms of Mr. Cherese, illustrated in the Ubirajara interview, only partly matched what I had heard previously. The following is what I learned from my sources prior to this interview:

1. Extreme chills, evidenced by his wife during a brief visit at his home.
2. Complaint of a backache.
3. Later developing fever, which became high and medically unmanageable.
4. Feelings of generalized malaise.
5. Superficial blood vessel engorgement, particularly involving the sclera of the eyes.
6. Skin rash.
7. Labored breathing.
8. Coma and death.

Since there was no written data available to me, I had no way to corroborate the authenticity of what I had heard. The testimony given by Dr. Cesario does in some way give credibility to what I heard previously. It is my impression the doctor is *not* telling the entire story. In looking at the blood scenario described by Dr. Cesario, I have come to the conclusion that there was indeed an overpowering infective organism. Perhaps this was not a bacterium at all, but a very potent virus. It also seems to me that there are certain parallels that can be drawn between Marco's symptoms and blood work and the possibility of an Ebola-like infection. I have also come to the conclusion that all medical personnel involved with the case did not want this to become public knowledge, as it might have caused widespread panic in the local population. I also believe because there was direct contact between Marco and the entity (he touched the being with an ungloved hand), that this could have been the portal of entry for the microorganism. The dermatologist referred to by Ubirajara in his questioning also suggested this same reasoning. If this were the case, then the portal of entry would be directly through the skin. Also, we must consider the age of the wound at the time of removal of the lesion in the armpit area. I have no way of knowing at this time whether it was the same arm used to touch the unknown entity.

There are other parts of the interview that seem to raise more questions. If there was such a good and open rapport between Dr. Cesario and the family, then why were their questions not answered by him personally? He admitted he knew Marco's sister. Why was she not given the details? Why was there such a delay in passing on a death certificate to the family? Why was the wife so intimidated that she could not answer any of my questions during my interview with her? I also question the doctor's opinion regarding how much knowledge could be ascertained from the exhumation of the corpse. This is a procedure done routinely here in the U.S. in a large number of criminal cases. There is much to be learned from this procedure. Perhaps this was not done because they were afraid to do it for fear of contamination and infection of others. I believe there will be NO forthcoming definitive answers regarding this death because the body will never be exhumed. How do we even know there is a body to exhume? Perhaps the corpse was cremated for safety reasons and the family was not told.

Chapter 15

FINAL SUMMARY

With my trip to Brazil at its end, I finished my last evening meal, excused myself from the dinner table and my friends, and told them I would be back. I exited the restaurant. The outside world was in utmost peace and a warm breeze was evident.

Compelled to walk, I went out into an open field and followed a few small trails which magically led me to a large, flat tree stump. It looked like a safe and comfortable place to sit, so that is what I did.

The warm air had the aroma of a primitive jungle. I tilted my head back and peered at the great expanse of starlit sky. So many stars and so clear!— perhaps due to the lack of light pollution in the area. I noticed the sky was different from what I was accustomed to viewing normally. The constellations were in different places. Suddenly I realized this was quite distinct from my home in California because I was in the Earth's southern hemisphere, offering a completely different angle of the sky.

I continued to sit and ponder, still gazing above. I began thinking that many creatures on this jungle floor were probably traversing the terrain below my feet, since earlier in the day I had seen one-inch sized brown ants carrying on their tasks. At the time I saw them they had not been aware of my alien presence on their turf, and just continued with their tasks by crossing my shoes.

The more I became engrossed in the heavenly scene spread before my eyes, the more thoughts surfaced on the Varginha case itself. Perhaps my new view of the night sky and of the heavens was somewhat similar to what was experienced in the minds of those non-terrestrial beings who found themselves stranded on this earth—far, far from their place of origin, knowing that they would never go home. Knowing that he would never return home could be the reason for the death of the creature operated on in Hospital Regional. He left the facility with a pronouncement that he was in satisfactory medical condition, only to be immediately taken to Humanitas Hospital, leaving there deceased, in a wooden box the following morning. Did he merely slip the bonds of this three-dimensional reality and join with the soul of Corporal Chereze in some dimension that we humans don't understand?

149

As I sat and pondered these facts, I realized that the Varginha, Brazil crash is the **single most important event** recorded and investigated in the entire UFO field to date. With the Roswell event of 1947 there had been an increasing number of witnesses who came forward in the past 50 years. The number has continued to diminish because of the age and death rate of the witnesses. In addition, the emphasis on the Roswell case is more on the recovery of a vehicle and the back-engineering of its advanced science, whereas in the Varginha case, we have increasing witnesses who have had interactions with actual beings from another world.

In August of 2004, for the first time ever, a conference was held in Varginha and was overseen by the various Brazilian investigators. They released more testimony about the case from new witnesses, some of which was detailed above. Although much of the information released at the conference was corroborative testimony, new information was presented such as what was revealed by the physician who actually treated the deceased military police officer, whose death was caused by direct exposure to one of the non-terrestrial beings. So for now, we are up to date on these events.

It is my unwavering and undoubting belief that this text, being an investigation into the absolute truth of these events, is one of the most important documents of the modern world and should be held in the highest esteem. Never before in the history of UFO investigations has there been such a great number of witnesses who had no relationship to each other and no motive for story-telling, who reported the same events with the same descriptions of the creatures involved. This is far beyond coincidence. Let me be the first to point out that there has been a number of great hoaxes previously perpetrated on various UFO researchers and the public in general, with some examples given in this text, however **THE VARGINHA CASE IS NO HOAX.**

CPSIA information can be obtained at www.ICGtesting.com
Printed in the USA
BVOW071406170313

315675BV00002B/201/A